Quit

Other Parenting Resources by AMBrewster

The *Truth.Love.Parent.* podcast

Biblical Parenting Essentials Conference

A Family United in God family worship series

The Year Long Celebration of God discipleship materials

Find all of these resources and more on the Evermind App. Scan the QR code to set up your free account.

"If you're frustrated with the way your home is filled with strife and discord, and you're wondering where this all might lead, this book offers the truthful answers you need. AMBrewster offers careful, biblical wisdom, first for discerning the true problem, then for responding in a way that causes strife—not to multiply—but melt away. Find out why self-focus creates strife and God-focus creates peace, and learn how to access God's power to put an end to the strife in your family circle."
    Shannon Popkin, wife, mother, author of *Shaped by God's Promises, Control Girl, and Comparison Girl* and host of the *Live Like It's True* Bible podcast

"I believe all Christian families can benefit from what Aaron addresses in this book. Through my years as a pastor, I have counseled countless families, and counseling never begins when things are good, but usually when things have gone very bad. Are there ways to keep from getting to that point? Yes, and that's what you will find in this book: Biblical answers to deal with the roots of strife and practical ways to stop this sinful infection from spreading within your family. Each chapter is focused on the timeless truths of Scripture, and the LifeWork exercises help to apply these truths practically to everyday life. This book is a must-read for anyone looking to strengthen their family's spiritual foundation. Whether you are facing challenges now or simply want to prevent future ones, this book provides the tools and guidance you need."
    Dr. M. Keith Foskey, husband, father, pastor, author of *God in Three Persons* and *A Biblically Functioning Church*, podcaster

"From the first sentence of this book to the last Aaron M. Brewster masterfully paints a picture of the reality that none of us can escape, while at the same time providing the hope of how to rise above it. If you have a family (or interact with any other person in your life) then you have relationships. If you have relationships, then you have strife. And since you have strife . . . you need this book in your collection! This short, yet mighty read is a powerful addition to the armor that God Himself provides us as we declare war against the *real* enemies in our lives: Satan, the World, and our own Flesh. The addition of Lifework and references to supportive resources are wonderful aspects as well. I believe the message of *Quit: How to Stop Family Strife for Good* was inspired directly from God and is able to meet each of us right where we are. Thank you, Aaron, for this labor of love that provides a relatable, concise, and easy to understand cure for the strife that daily ensnares our families!!!"
    Cara Belcastro, wife, mother, and second grade teacher

Quit

How to Stop Family Strife for Good

AMBrewster

Quit: How to Stop Family Strife for Good

Copyright ©2024 by Aaron M. Brewster.

Published by Evermind Publishing
   53 Cherry St.
   Brevard, NC 28712

All rights reserved. No portion of this book may be reproduced in any form without written permission from the publisher or author, except as permitted by U.S. copyright law.

Book Cover and Illustrations: AMBrewster
Cover image: Adobe Stock #480588739, stock.adobe.com, Aerial drone view of Vidraru dam in Romania by frimufilms

1st edition 2024

Unless otherwise indicated, scripture quotations are from The ESV® Bible (The Holy Bible, English Standard Version®), copyright© 2001 by Crossway. Used by permission. All rights reserved.

Scripture quotations marked (NASB 1995) taken from the (NASB®) New American Standard Bible®, Copyright © 1995 by The Lockman Foundation. Used by permission. All rights reserved. lockman.org.

Scripture quotations marked (NASB) taken from the (NASB®) New American Standard Bible®, Copyright © 2020 by The Lockman Foundation. Used by permission. All rights reserved. lockman.org

Trade Paperback ISBN: 979-8-9909785-0-8

Special thanks to a young man
without whom this book
would likely never have been written.

And grateful appreciation for
all the members of Truth.Love.Family.
who have waited so patiently for it.

Contents

Introduction 11

Part 1: The Creators of Strife

1. Three Strife Creators in Your Home 17

2. Six More Strife Creators in Your Home 25

Part 2: The Consequences of Strife

3. Sin Hurts 37

Part 3: The Causes of Strife

4. Deliberate Unbelief 49

5. Immaturity & Fleshly Living 57

Part 4: The Cure for Strife

6. Trust the Truth & Submit to the Spirit 69

7. Grow in God 83

8. Quit the Strife 93

Conclusion 103

Nobody Needs an **Introduction** to Strife.

The seeds of this book were planted back when I worked at a boys home for at risk teens. It was our second year, and we had a young man who lit relational fires everywhere he went. I tried diligently to help him, but so much of my counsel fell on deaf ears because he saw everyone else as the problem. One day, while reading through Proverbs, I repeatedly encountered various descriptions of strife Creators, and I couldn't help but see this young man in *every description*. But it was also in the descriptions that I started to see God's plan for extinguishing family strife for good. When I discovered Proverbs 17:14, God's Cure for strife all made sense, "The beginning of strife is like letting out water, so **quit** before the quarrel breaks out" (emphasis mine).

So, I copied all of the passages onto a piece of paper and asked the young man to read them. By God's grace, that was the start of a study we did together that not only eventually helped him turn a relational corner, but also grow into the book you're holding in your hands right now.

Though I was able to enjoy the fruit it produced in that young man, what I didn't know was how pivotal that study would be in me as I moved from teaching others what the Bible said about strife to actually believing it for myself. It was during that same year at the boys home that strife exploded into one of my closest friendships. I had not ever experienced that level of pain, and we were on an utterly destructive trajectory. Thankfully, the story doesn't have a tragic end. I can confidently proclaim with Paul "but God!" (Ephesians 2:4). From the world's perspective, our relationship was doomed to toxic failure, *but God* through His mercy and grace had a different plan. He desired for us to be changed and reconciled, and the principles I discuss in this book were at the heart of that plan.

But I know for certain that my life is not the only one plagued by strife. Did you know the very first recorded family conflict involved God and His very own creation? This conflict occurred when the first humans sinned against God and then hid themselves in disgrace. The second recorded conflict transpired hours later when the first husband blamed his wife for the sin *he* had committed. The third conflict resulted when the first son committed the first murder. Sadly, families throughout the ages (including the Brewsters) have willfully continued this shameful tradition. The takeaway here is to see that the moment sin entered the world, strife ensued.

The Merriam-Webster dictionary defines strife as "bitter, sometimes violent conflict or dissension" and "an act of contention: fight, struggle." Families experience strife in their homes almost daily. Strife ruins meals, shatters silence, and derails fun. This is because fighting, quarreling, and competing amongst children have become the norm in most houses.

However, strife-making is not at all limited to our children; even as parents, we can create daily conflict within our families. Looking back, I can so easily see what I couldn't (or didn't want to) see then—I was at the very epicenter of our family's strife, and far too often I saw it as everyone else's fault!

It should come as no surprise then that parent-child conflict is so common in today's world that it has become cliché. If a parent and teenager get along, if a two-year-old doesn't have temper tantrums, if a middle-school child accepts reproof without arguing, and if parents aren't in a state of perpetual anger or anxiety, the family is considered an enigma. But why should strife seem normal while peace appears strange? Perhaps it's due to the fact that family peace is so hard to attain. This should cause us to ask whether it's even possible to reduce the level of strife in our homes, or—better yet—remove the strife for good.

Thankfully, God didn't leave us to live in continuous strife. His perfect Word provides all the guidance and direction our families need for a life of godliness *and strifelessness.* To begin moving toward strifelessness in our families, we will wade into the book of Proverbs and study three New Testament epistles to discover the *Creators, Consequences,* and *Causes* of strife, and then uncover the *Cures.*

Why not simply start with the Cures? I'm convinced we must first *understand* truth in order to apply it correctly. I once asked a mechanic to replace my car's transmission, but he wisely ran a diagnostic test first. After running the test, he discovered my transmission only needed reprogramming. No one wants to pay to overhaul his car's transmission without first determining the real issue, so I was very grateful the mechanic was honest. Likewise, trying to "fix" a family without a biblical diagnostic is just as foolish. This is why we must be thorough in our acquisition of knowledge and biblical insight. Here's what we're going to learn:

- Part 1 is about the Creators of strife. The Bible introduces us to nine human character traits that always cause strife, and we must carefully identify the individuals in our homes who have these characteristics.
- Part 2 is designed to show us that even though strife may be culturally acceptable, it's Consequences are so incredibly destructive. Strife affects every relationship and stains every experience, and it's imperative that we understand why it hurts so much.
- Part 3 dives into the Causes at the very foundation of our strife-creating character and teaches us to identify those Causes in us and our kids.
- Part 4 presents God's Cure for family strife by teaching us to incrementally remove the Causes, thus impacting the character of the Creators, and thereby avoiding the Consequences of this ugly thing called strife.

Knowledge and understanding, however, are not the only prerequisites to change. It's vital we apply what we've learned. Sprinkled throughout the chapters, you'll discover what I like to call "LifeWork." No one likes homework, but everyone wants a better life. The LifeWork sections provide an opportunity for practical application of the material. These sections include relevant questions to help you consider and understand your family's unique needs, along with detailed action steps you can add to your daily parenting. Responding carefully to the LifeWork questions will provide valuable insight into the problems facing your family, prompting practical answers to guide you toward solutions.

I pray these life-changing truths will equip you to experience reconciliation and relief from your family's strife-induced pain. I believe this may be the first step toward your family quitting the strife for good!

Always,

AMBrewster

Part 1
The Creators of Strife

1
Three Strife Creators in Your Home

Dam failure is a catastrophic event. It's so destructive that laws of honorable military conduct prohibit soldiers from targeting enemy dams due to the resulting horrific civilian casualties and mass devastation of infrastructure. I once witnessed a relatively small dam in Michigan's Upper Peninsula empty into the Menominee River. It was terrifying to watch thousands of gallons of water explode through the spillway with a deafening roar—and that was a very small, *controlled* release!

Consider the metaphor we read earlier in Proverbs 17:14, "The beginning of strife is like letting out water." The English translation of "letting out water" doesn't quite capture the full picture. Imagine, instead, a giant dam cracking and splitting. Which element of the picture do you think best illustrates strife? Could it be the broken dam? Maybe strife is illustrated by the water? This verse provides the answer by telling us that strife *begins* when the water is "let out." The strife, therefore, is neither the water nor the broken dam. Strife is most comparable to the actual *destruction* the torrent of raging water creates as it bursts through the dam. And remember, many raging torrents begin with only a little release of water.

In the Proverbs metaphor, I believe the dam best represents our self-control, and the water depicts our sinful nature—all the pride, selfishness, bitterness, dishonesty, hate, lustful thoughts, gossip, impatience, gluttony, and rebelliousness swirling around in our minds. Our culturally acceptable facade (the dam wall) keeps our worst elements hidden, but when our self-control breaks, the ugliest parts of our hearts explode all over the closest person. As that torrent of wickedness pours out onto them, it leaves nothing but relational destruction.

That is strife.

In the same way a levee full of water can create far more destruction than the pond behind a beaver dam; the more sin we have pent up in our lives, the greater the potential for strife. However, we probably need to update our illustration a bit for it to be more biblically accurate. In truth, sin is less like water and more like acid. Unlike the subtle relationship between the water and the concrete barrier, sin actively *eats away* at our self-control, compromising the very integrity of our dam walls. We absolutely cannot contain sin by building thicker walls because the more immature and obsessed we are with ourselves, the faster our self-control will crumble, releasing a torrent of strife on those around us.

So, for the sake of this study, when I talk about strife, I'm referring to the consequences of sin in our relationships. But where does strife originate?

People Cause Strife

People ultimately cause strife, so it's impossible to remove strife without addressing the personalities involved. This is why we must take special note of each family member. Knowing who the different types of strife Creators are is imperative to applying God's Cure for strife in your home. This chapter and the next will analyze the types of people with the most significant potential for creating strife.

Identifying these strife Creators is immensely valuable as it highlights the particular types of acidic sin possessing the greatest potential for creating strife. People who fit these categories have vast amounts of strife-causing potential hidden behind the walls of their lives. All sin needs to explode across the room is a crack in our self-control as we succumb to temptation.

Later in the book, there will be specific information that will apply uniquely to the nine types of strife Creators and instructions for removing strife from your home. First, however, you must identify the *individual* conflict Creators in your house so you'll be able to apply God's Cure for strife specifically and accurately to your family's unique needs.

Now, I know that this will be difficult for some of us. We all desperately love our kids no matter how much strife they're creating, but some of you may think that labeling your children as "strife Creators" or identifying the ways they sin is unloving. My friends, that is not the case. The most loving thing we can do for our children is to help them better know God, understand themselves, and live in accordance with God's will for their lives. It's not unloving to identify the sinful choices that breed strife in your marriage, it's actually most unloving to ignore them. I know you love your family members, and that's why I know you want to help them love the Lord and love everyone else in your home by limiting their sin and reducing the strife.

So, with that said, it's important to know that the following list of character traits is structured to grow in two ways:

1. The categories move from specific to general, and . . .

2. The categories appear to progress from most egregious to culturally benign. In reality, however, *all sin* is deplorable before God's holy gaze.

Those of you with young children (or kids who "have a good heart") may be tempted to skip ahead past the seemingly "aggressive" nature of the first few categories to the more "applicable" sins of childhood. I challenge you, though, to look carefully at your children—*every* category can apply to children of any age.

1. Addicts Stir Up Strife

This category may seem intense or irrelevant to your home situation, but there is something in this section that applies to *all* families. The book of Proverbs definitively points out this type of strife creator:

> Who has woe? Who has sorrow? Who has strife? Who has complaining? Who has wounds without cause? Who has redness of eyes? [30] Those who tarry long over wine; those who go to try mixed wine (Proverbs 23:29-30).

Millions of Americans are addicted to drinking alcohol,[1] resulting in mangled relationships and devastated bodies. I start with this type of strife Creator because it's so relevant to our culture.

While working at Victory Academy for Boys, there were many at-risk teens who moved into our home who had used and abused alcohol. Most of these kids were introduced to alcohol by their peers, but countless children worldwide have been introduced to alcohol via their parents' casual drinking habits. It doesn't take long for children (and parents) in such homes to start crossing the line, from warming their throats to feeling buzzed to getting drunk.

This principle, however, applies to more than just alcohol abuse because there will always be strife when you get between an addict and his or her fix. This truth applies to alcohol, technology, drugs, and even coffee. Unfortunately, it's depressingly easy to become addicted to even the most benign things like toys, work, television, and social media. *Anything* we think we need to be satisfied but don't biblically need is an addiction.

Some addictions, like substance abuse, inherently provoke strife by changing the user on a physiological level. Stand in the way of the addict and her chocolate, however, and you're asking for an equally ferocious fight! The same goes for those addicted to gaming, sleeping, exercising, or reading. It's also as true for a parent who's being a dictator to his children as it is for a five-year-old who refuses to eat her vegetables. The reason for this is that addiction to our own pleasure functions very much like physical dependence.

When dealing with addicted people, two basic traits need to be understood. Firstly, addicts will willingly sacrifice what is truly valuable for the far less valuable short-term gain—when your daughter throws her broccoli on the ground, she's willing to sacrifice her fellowship with Mom to keep a "bad" taste out of her mouth. The second trait addicts exhibit is

---

[1] Awareness, Alcohol. 2022. "How Many People Suffer from Alcohol Addiction?" AlcoholAwareness.org. June 10, 2022. Accessed January 8, 2023. https://alcoholawareness.org/how-many-people-suffer-from-alcohol-addiction/.

withdrawal. This occurs when an addict is deprived of a fix—upon being told to eat her vegetables, this child, who until that point in her life, has likely been spared genuine cruelties and been filled with little other than joyous opportunities, experiences a deep sense of loss and emptiness. Tears and anger explode from her. Is a toddler an addict? Has their addiction been revealed because of broccoli? Yes, and I will explain how shortly. For now, please understand that this behavior is a typical sign of withdrawal.

Addiction is a wide-ranging and complex topic, too vast to cover in this section, but it's vital to understand that addictions to physical substances or life patterns are merely *secondary* addictions. The *primary* addiction is far more insidious. You may remember the conversation we had on the Truth.Love.Parent (TLP) podcast episode entitled, *Is Your Child Addicted? Yes!* Not only did we learn all about our child's addiction, we also found their primary addiction is far more destructive than mere heroin or sex could ever be.

Be aware that if you have addicts in your home, be they addicted to substances, emotions, or self, there will be strife in the house.

Is Your Child Addicted?

2. God-Haters Stir Up Strife

To identify the following type of strife Creator, we return to the book of Proverbs where we read: "Drive out a scoffer, and strife will go out" (Proverbs 22:10). The Hebrew word for "scoffer" in this verse is *lûṣ*,[2] and is synonymous with "scorner," referring to a person who not only rejects, but also mocks and derides God's truth. This scoffer is known for outwardly showing hatred for God, His Word, and His people.

Most people cringe at the word "hate" because, as a culture, we've defined it incorrectly for so long. When discussing biblical hatred in this point and the next, it will be beneficial for you to realize that sinful hatred is simply the fruit of selfishness and the opposite of love. Where love is the desire to work toward the highest spiritual good of others, sinful hatred is wanting and working toward *our own* fleshly comfort *above* others. This definition stands whether we're discussing hatred toward God, family members, or people from other ethnicities.

This isn't to say that every word and action of a God-hater creates contention. I've known many atheists and scoffers who were often quite pleasant individuals, but it's impossible for a God-denier not to create strife to some degree or another. If you bring up the topic of God or contradict

---

[2] H3887 – *lûṣ* – Strong's Hebrew Lexicon

their worldview, havoc and destruction eventually ensue in the relationship. When the unbeliever encounters a trial, they *must* choose to disobey God because their worldview opposes all God is. Even their "good" behavior, gifted to them by common grace, is sinful because it is done for their own glory instead of God's. This is true of unbelievers of every age because when seemingly good behavior is planted in selfish soil, even the most beautiful plant bears bitter fruit.

Scripture tells us that living in selfishness is hostility toward God. Indeed, children born into the world haven't learned to submit to God and therefore start as rebellious and hostile toward God: "For the mind that is set on the flesh is hostile to God, for it does not submit to God's law; indeed, it cannot. [8] Those who are in the flesh cannot please God" (Romans 8:7-8). Until they submit to Him and His truth, each child is solidly in enemy territory—a few small steps away from being a scorner.

It's regrettable, but there's a certain degree to which we're comfortable with the strife infants cause because "They're just babies." Seasoned parents with more than one child, however, can tell you precisely when their bundles of joy *consciously* decided to disobey for the first time.

To illustrate this, my parents tell a story of my then six-month-old sister standing in her crib, laughing, and "talking" when she should have been sleeping. My father refused to allow her disobedience, but my mother pleaded on her behalf, saying, "She doesn't know what she's doing. She's just a baby!" My mother learned a valuable lesson one night as she tried to coddle the laughing baby to sleep. My sister heard the steps of my frustrated father approaching her room and immediately lay prostrate on her pillow, feigning sleep! My six-month-old sister had *consciously refused* to heed my mother's pleas but selfishly "obeyed" when she realized consequences were about to arrive.

I know this can be a hard pill to swallow, but if we as parents accept the self-worship of our infants, we'll also be tempted to excuse the idolatry of our toddlers. I know it may sound extreme to some, but we must ask ourselves, "At what age should godliness begin?" I've met too many parents who dismiss sin in their children because they were children, but all of a sudden (at a subjective point chosen by the parents), these same dads and moms no longer have patience for the child's sin. They finally decide their child is "old enough" to know better, and the foolishness and disobedience are no longer tolerated. Yet the teen isn't necessarily more selfish than the toddler; it's simply that the parents no longer view their teenaged child's disobedience as "cute." We'll suppress laughter when our five-year-old steals cookies and denies it with crumb-covered lips, but no one laughs or takes pictures when their tween sneaks money out of their wallet. We don't have patience for a self-worshipper in middle school like we did when they were in preschool. But those are subjective responses. They're not biblical.

The hard reality is that until a child is born again, they are estranged from God and incapable of pleasing Him. Even the noblest acts they perform are sinful, as we see in Proverbs 21:4, "An high look, and a proud heart, and the plowing of the wicked, is sin" (KJV). Even while the unsaved farmer works hard to steward his land and care for his family efficiently, he's sinning. How can this be? It's because a terrorist is still an enemy of the state even when he's rocking his baby daughter to sleep. That unbelieving farmer doesn't care about God, so he doesn't work his land and provide for His family to the glory of God. Scripture tells us that since the farmer's motivation is wrong, he's sinning: "Whether, then, you eat or drink or whatever you do, do all to the glory of God" (I Corinthians 10:31). Everything the scorner or scoffer does is accompanied by a refusal to accept the Gospel; therefore strife will be inherent even in their "good works."

A perfect example of this was my experience with an unsaved girl who moved to the school where I was an associate administrator. She was a fantastic student and a generally fun person with whom to spend time, but since her overachievement was motivated by selfish desire, she struggled with anxiety over her grades. The girl fell into depression when she didn't fare as well as she would have liked and exuded pride when she did. If she felt mistreated by her friends, she became furious and was so emotionally unstable that few people wanted to associate with her in or out of class.

The vital lesson we must learn is that sin always causes strife, and those who reject God (the root of all sins) have strife creeping around every corner. If you have any unbelievers in your household, you will have strife.

3. Hateful People Stir Up Strife

"Hatred stirs up strife. . ." (Proverbs 10:12).

This proverb may seem like an obvious statement, but hate is an equal-opportunity life choice, so the people who reject God's salvation aren't the only ones causing strife. Bearing in mind that sinful hatred is simply the fruit of selfishness and the opposite of love, worshiping myself and being willing to sacrifice you to get what I want is selfish and, indeed, the very definition of sinful hate. It goes without saying that if I hate you, there *will* be conflict—especially if you're willing to sacrifice me to achieve your objective. This is true even among born-again Christians.

It's too bad that salvation doesn't instantly rid us of selfishness, but that was never God's plan prior to glory. Learning to sacrifice our desires to accomplish the Lord's will comes from growth in maturity. This is why the automatic response of the immature is all-consuming selfishness. There is a distinct path from childish hatred to the adult form of selfish hatefulness that is easy to detect once you know where to look:

1. At birth, an infant doesn't have the capacity to consider any needs beyond his own. Mom, Dad, and siblings spend all their time catering to the little bundle, and though it would be sinful not to care for the baby, we've all experienced the strife caused by an inconsolable child. Despite the fact that it's extremely uncomfortable to suggest our infants "hate us," we need to accept at least that they don't possess the ability to experience *agapē*[3] (true love) for us. They may have bucket loads of *storgē*[4]—the natural familial affection inherent in humans—but they cannot choose to do anything in another's best interest. An infant cannot decide, "Mother, you sleep in today. I can wait another hour before eating, and I promise not to spit up on you because I know how stressful that is for you."
2. When a child begins to walk, the immature toddler slowly becomes aware that other people exist but doesn't really care about their desires, even when serving another could benefit the toddler. Instead of sharing a toy with his sibling in an attempt to engender a lasting relationship, the toddler lacks the ability to see beyond his momentary passions. As he snatches the toy from his brother, conflict ensues. This immature selfishness offers an accurate illustration of sinful hatred.
3. As the child's mind grows, the ten-year-old selfishly develops the ability to imagine more convincing ways to accomplish her own desires. Her growing lack of biblical love for others (also known as hatred) drives her to try out these new ways to obtain what she wants. Compounding her selfishness with the fact that her self-worship is no longer culturally cute, her clumsy manipulations do little more than elicit arguments and quarreling within the home.
4. When these immature children become teenagers, they can be the savviest manipulators. Many of them have mastered the ability to please their flesh while *appearing* to please others. This tends to increase the level of strife for various reasons:
    - By the time this idolater becomes a teenager, most family members have reached their last nerve.
    - Failed manipulation attempts do little more than provoke negative responses from everyone else in the family.
    - "Successful" manipulation strengthens the teen's self-worship, exponentially increasing the potential for strife.

---

[3] "G26 – *agapē* – Strong's Greek Lexicon"

[4] "G5387 - Philostorgos - Strong's Greek Lexicon (KJV)." n.d. Blue Letter Bible. Accessed January 9, 2023. https://www.blueletterbible.org/lexicon/g5387/kjv/tr/0-1/.

- If that "successful" manipulation is later revealed, it too often results in hateful responses from other family members.
5. On the other hand, children aren't the only ones who behave hatefully in our families. Too often, Dad uses his stressful job to justify unlovingly ignoring his children. And which mom hasn't wanted to retaliate in word or deed against the ever-present siphons in her life? Even though we want so badly to justify our screaming and manipulating, we must face the fact that such behavior grows out of self-love. As with the previous two types of strife Creators discussed, hateful (selfish) people living in your home will cause strife.

For those of you who are serious about moving toward the cure for strife in your home, I encourage you to re-listen to TLP's discussion on Family Love to better understand love and see hatred the way God defines it. *The Four Family Loves* series starts with a discussion of biblical hate, looks at the four types of family love, and concludes with several episodes detailing various implications of living in true love.

The Four Family Loves

Having now covered the first three types of people who cause strife, in the next chapter, we will examine six more strife causers. These nine character traits will provide you with a complete picture of the possible sources of strife in your home. You'll find your first LifeWork assignment at the end of chapter 2. There you'll be asked to identify the sinful character traits in each of your family members. For now, though, you can be certain that everyone in your family struggles with the primary addiction of self. We all do. Every single one of our sins is rooted in our incessant drive to please ourselves and do what's right in our own eyes.

But what about hatred? If you're reading this book, then you've likely seen plenty of unloving behavior in your home. Don't allow the theoretical descriptions of these character traits to distract from the fact that many—if not most—of them are alive and well in your family. Identifying the Creators of strife is a necessary step to implementing the Cure.

2
Six More Strife Creators in Your Home

Are you prone to being hot-tempered, angry, wrathful, or argumentative? Is your spouse a dishonest person? Are your children greedy? Most people, especially believers, don't think they or their family members habitually fall prey to these strife-creating sins. Lord willing, this chapter will open your eyes to some startling biblical realities. While the previous chapter dealt with what might be considered the three most abominable strife Creators, this chapter covers those strife-creating sins that should be more easily recognizable in every family. This will provide you with a complete picture of the possible sources of strife in your home, but please bear in mind that all sins are equally dangerous.

Believe it or not, every page of this chapter is relevant to your family. Recognizing the following six strife Creators occurring in every family will be critical to finding the Cure for strife in your own family. These sins are not graded on a scale from more significant to lesser—they all create strife! Consider carefully then where these six character traits may be found in your home.

4. Greedy People Stir Up Strife

This first passage about greed is almost identical to a verse we discussed when considering hateful people: "A greedy man stirs up strife" (Proverbs 28:25). The verse about hatred says, "Hatred stirs up strife. . . ." (Proverbs 10:12). The similarity of these verses pertains to the fact that greed grows on the branch of hatred, which in turn springs from the trunk of selfishness.

How do I reach this pithy conclusion? Remember that sinful hatred is the fruit of selfishness and the opposite of love. Sinful hatred is wanting and working toward our *own* fleshly interest above others. So, if I care for my comfort above yours, I'll hate you while I search greedily for what makes me happy. Then, as I strive to be satisfied outside of God's will, I will inevitably crave those things I don't have but think I need.

In keeping with our tree metaphor, greed is the veritable blossom of discontentment. The greedy person covets the objects they desire, hoping they will bring contentment. But the Bible teaches that only selflessness which grows from *agapē* love—brings contentment. Let's see these truths in action:

- Remember that unloving toddler who took his brother's toy? He coveted the toy because he cared more about his own pleasure, feeling convinced his sibling's toy would satisfy him.

- Siblings playing a video game system argue so passionately because they want to win, and they viciously envy their sibling's digital gold medal, skill, or pure dumb luck.
- Our culture loves to feed our discontentment, which creates fertile ground for covetousness. This greed supplies never-ending demands for the newest styles, tech, shows, and music. This same ploy is also the siren call of the drug culture. Everything designed for teens tries to convince them they need something else to be happy. When prepubescent hedonists are denied their lusts, what happens? Strife.
- Have you ever watched a greedy parent? Some adults will sacrifice their children's health and well-being for material possessions, while other parents are jealous of their neighbors' income or their friends' cherubic children. Some parents are greedy for the approval of others and do their best to have a picture-perfect family—not for God's glory, but to fulfill their lusts. Discontentment always breeds greed, and greed always gives birth to strife.

Be on guard against all ingratitude and discontentment in your home. Wherever you find greed, you will find strife.

5. Dishonest People Stir Up Strife

Addicts, scoffers, haters, and greedy people aren't the only strife Creators in our homes. Proverbs 16:28 tells us, "A dishonest man spreads strife, and a whisperer separates close friends."

Remember, this list of strife-creating character traits is designed to help us understand a simple truth: *all* of our homes will have strife because they all have *people* in them. The list, however, is also designed to open our eyes to the *specific* needs of our unique families. Be aware that this information will be invaluable when we examine the *Cures* for strife.

For now, though, we must recognize that dishonesty is a *sneaky* strife-starter. Sometimes the strife caused by dishonesty is delayed, sometimes it's immediate, and sometimes it's imminent.

- Poor, immature liars are easy to catch, and the strife results from the one lying, the one to whom they lied, or both.
- Savvy liars are harder to catch, but—since lies always hurt the liar—strife will creep through regardless. When the lie is finally revealed, the water starts *gushing* through this crack in the dam.
- The most challenging part of living with a liar is never knowing when they're lying. This challenge creates strife even when the person may not have told a lie!

If you have dishonest people in your house, you will encounter daily strife.

6. Hot-Tempered/Angry/Argumentative People Stir Up Strife
Do you have a child or a spouse with a short fuse? How's your own temper? Let's see what scripture says about wrath and anger:

Proverbs 15:18: "A hot-tempered man stirs up strife."

Proverbs 29:22: "A man of wrath stirs up strife, and one given to anger causes much transgression."

Proverbs 30:33: "For pressing milk produces curds, pressing the nose produces blood, and pressing anger produces strife."

Proverbs 26:21: "As charcoal to hot embers and wood to fire, so is a quarrelsome man for kindling strife."

All of our daily experiences reveal this category to be pretty obvious. Hot-tempered, angry, argumentative people create strife *all the time*. Strife may be a by-product of many of the character issues we've seen, but this quarrelsome individual *deliberately* creates conflict. They want strife to rip through the person at whom they're angry.

- It grievously saddens me that sinful anger is a stereotype of fatherhood. What saddens me even more is how a wrathful and vitriolic diva has replaced a previous stereotype of the sweet and demure mother. There's hardly a sitcom, reality show, movie, or book where the parents aren't constantly angry. This shift in our entertainment is merely a reflection of our cultural reality.
- Of course, teenage angst is also depressingly expected in our culture. A happy teen is considered so abnormal they seem suspicious.
- Although most elementary and toddler-aged kids usually aren't labeled as having short tempers and rage problems, we almost expect our kids will throw tantrums because "that's what kids do."

Anger is a sick symptom of a godless culture. At the time of this writing, an outright war is being waged promoting abortion, transgenderism, and aberrant sexuality of every kind, and the primary weapon brandished in this conflict is neither logic, reason, nor information . . . it's *wrath*. Social media has become a firestorm of abuse for anyone trying to engage these issues from a biblical standpoint. Mobs are rioting and looting because they're not getting the political results they want.

I'm expounding on this because the world sees anger as a *legitimate* way of dealing with conflict, and the world is influencing your family. I remember watching *Sesame Stree*t as a young boy, noticing how an animated goat reacted whenever people were unkind to him: "I get mad, I get mad, I get mad. It ain't bad to get mad!" It has stuck with me to this day. Of course, there is a level of truth to this, as the first part of Ephesians 4:26 says, "Be angry and do not sin . . ." but I recommend you trust the Word of God over *Sesame Street* for the full picture. We all get angry, but the key is *not to sin* while doing it. The second half of Ephesians 4:26 gives you a clue regarding how to avoid such sin. It says, ". . . do not let the sun go down on your anger." We need to control our anger and never let it linger, or it will fester into sin.

The need for education regarding dealing biblically with wrathful kids is evident in that one of TLP's most popular series is *Parenting Angry Children*. Those episodes not only seek to biblically define each category of sinful anger, but also help parents understand the nature and cure for anger. If you have angry people in your home, you will have strife.

Parenting Angry Children

7. Prideful, Arrogant People Stir Up Strife

Scripture reveals this significant truth in this way: "By insolence comes nothing but strife" (Proverbs 13:10). Insolence isn't quite the best translation for this Hebrew word. The English word "insolence" refers to being rude, impolite, or disrespectful, but the Hebrew word refers to pride, presumptuousness, and arrogance. It shouldn't be surprising that pride causes strife because it's frequently referred to as the root of all sin. How can arrogant people *not* cause strife?

Here are a few truths about arrogance within families:
- Arrogance and pride are generally not words we use when describing infants and toddlers, but don't be fooled. Remember our tree metaphor, "Greed grows on the branch of hatred which springs from the trunk of selfishness"? Well, connected to that trunk are the roots of pride. Infants are inherently greedy, selfish, and unloving. As infants, they don't know any other way. Their greed, selfishness, and lack of love grow from the same place ours does . . . pride.
- Arrogant behavior is becoming increasingly prevalent among our elementary and middle-school kids. As young athletes idolize professional players, they find impersonating their idol's ego easier than his or her athletic prowess. Also, many more children listen to music and watch movies with progressively mature content. The music industry, in particular, is a veritable arrogance factory, and it's doing its best to manufacture pride across the globe.
- When these kids hit puberty, they sometimes blossom well, and the attention they receive feeds their pride. Meanwhile, the other 70% manifest their pride by lamenting the fact they don't look the way they'd like.
- What about mom and dad? Our biggest hurdle is quite often the arrogant thought we "deserve" something simply because we're

mom and dad. The idea that parents deserve respect, obedience, and enviable children is nothing more than pride.

And what happens when we live and breathe in an atmosphere of arrogance? Generally, there are two consequences:

1. We don't tolerate anyone who doesn't worship us to the same degree we worship ourselves.
2. Since no one else is interested in worshipping us, they refuse to submit to our dictatorships.

Our *Family Worship* series is a wonderful counterpart to this discussion because it details the various types of pride that deceive us into thinking we don't have to worship God.

If you have prideful people living in your home, you will definitely have strife.

***

So, we've made it this far. According to the first seven character traits, how's your family doing? Do you have any addicts? Are there any haters in the house? How about greedy, dishonest, angry, or prideful people? Given the character issues represented in your home, do you think there may be some strife today? If, however, these flaws somehow cannot be found in your family (yeah, right), I regret to inform you the last two are unavoidable.

Family Worship

8. Fools Stir Up Strife

Scripture states: "It is an honor for a man to keep aloof from strife, but every fool will be quarreling" (Proverbs 20:3). Although pride covers a broad scope of behavior, foolishness is even more comprehensive. We know all children have foolishness knotted up within their being because God provides us a glimpse into our children's hearts: "Foolishness is bound up in the heart of a child; The rod of discipline will remove it far from him" (Proverbs 22:15, NASB). Here, we are given a divine guarantee there *will* be strife in our home *simply because children are present*.

It's not just children, though. You would hope that foolishness decreases as age increases, but the reality seems to be the opposite. Why do we parents so readily say and do the things we know from experience will only create strife? Because we're fools. Like dogs returning to their vomit, we return to our asinine parenting.

Parenting a Zombie

I like to refer to this foolishness as "zombie behavior" because it mindlessly chomps away at everything important, regardless of the personal pain people endure. I wrote a whole series on *Parenting a Zombie* because all our children are born into the world as fools. If we don't address it early and often, the situation will only worsen.

If you have a fool in your home, there will be strife.

9. Sinful People Stir Up Strife

This final point should make it painfully apparent that there will be strife as long as we have sinners *of any kind* in our home. Both the Old and New Testaments make this clear:

"Whoever loves transgression loves strife; he who makes his door high seeks destruction" (Proverbs 17:19). This verse identifies the consequence of sin, and the next identifies the people who sin. "For all have sinned and come short of the glory of God" (Romans 3:23).

To transgress means to cross over or go beyond the bounds of something. In this particular example, we've all transgressed God's commands. This transgression is called sin, an unavoidable spiritual and genetic trait that permeates all we do. There will always be some amount of sinfully acidic water behind our dams because we'll all be sinners until we die or Christ returns.

Hopefully, that acid level will slowly decrease as we become more like Christ, but it will always be there to one degree or another. Because you have sinners in your home, *you will eventually have strife*.

In conclusion to this rather somber chapter, let's review the important takeaways:

1. Sin exists in all of us. That means we don't love God and others as we should but instead love ourselves far too much. That causes us to pridefully fight for our own way, which is foolish and often results in envy, lying, and anger when we don't get what we want. This behavior betrays the fact that we're desperately addicted to our own pleasure.
2. Strife results from us giving in to temptation and allowing our sin to influence our words and actions. The only way to successfully reduce family strife is to reduce the amount of sin in the family.
3. The best way to help your family grow *away* from sin is to pinpoint how each of you struggles, understand the Consequences of those choices, and then address the root Cause of your sin.

LifeWork Project

Write the names of everyone in your family (including your own), and see if you can pinpoint at least two categories from the list below that show up in your lives the most. If you can easily add more categories to each name, go right ahead! However, don't only scribble "sinner" for everyone—try to choose from the more specific categories first.

Strife Creators: addicts, God-haters, people-haters, greedy people, liars, angry people, prideful people, fools, and sinners.

_____

_____

_____

_____

_____

_____

_____

_____

_____

_____

_____

_____

_____

_____

_____

A Self-Focus Creates Strife

There's one more crucial foundation stone to consider before we move to our next point. Parenting, discipleship, and counseling are experiences that either create strife or introduce peace. There is no middle ground. Think about that for a moment. If how I relate to the people in my life flows from who *I am* and what *I want* to accomplish, then my relational approach is self-focused and self-motivated. In that case, I know the following is true:

1. I'm addicted to my own desires.
2. I'm not loving God because I'm not obeying God.
3. I'm not loving the people in my life because I'm not relating to them in the best way I can.
4. I'm desperately covetous for my own way.
5. I'm being dishonest with the people in my life about how we're meant to live our lives.
6. I'm likely to become easily angered when I don't get the results I desire.
7. All this ultimately flows from being a prideful, arrogant individual who chooses to relate to the people in my life however I want to, despite what God says.
8. Biblically speaking, this prideful arrogance makes me a fool.
9. Every one of these responses is sinful, and all eight of them are strife Creators.

However . . .

A God-Focus Creates Peace

When I humbly submit to God's expectations for my life, I'm being wise, and I'm creating an atmosphere for peace to thrive.

1. If I'm passionate about how God wants me to relate to the people in my life,
2. If I'm giving the Lord the love due to Him by obeying His expectations for my relationships,
3. If I'm loving everyone by relating to them in the best way I possibly can—better than I could ever muster through my own strength,
4. If I do this because I'm zealous for God's way,
5. If I'm honest with everyone about how God wants me and them to live,
6. And if I don't become easily angered . . .
7. Because it's not about me,
8. I'm being wise,

9. And, therefore, I'm fleeing sin and running toward righteousness . . .

. . . then strife will never flow from my life.

    I mention all of this here because it's quite natural for us to try to start applying what we're learning as we move through each chapter. Now that we've learned about the nine character traits that create strife and identified which family members struggle with which sins, it's expected that we will start addressing these issues when we see them. However, if we're not careful to do it the right way, the very act of trying to work with the strife Creators will cause it's own strife as we do it in our own power for our own glory, and that will multiply the unavoidable Consequences of strife.

    In the next chapter we'll learn how Consequences affect us, how to use the moments stained by strife to better identify the strife Creators, and how God wants to use the Consequences of strife to help us and our families. I used to think that the pain that came from conflict was an absolute waste until I learned that God is powerful enough to redeem those experiences and turn them into a vital ingredient in my own spiritual maturity.

Part 2

The Consequences of Strife

3
Sin Hurts

Sin hurts. This is one of the greatest lessons everyone in your family must learn. Those strife-creating character traits hurt not only us, but also everyone around us. A father cannot sin without affecting his entire home, and this is equally true for the toddler. Sin is the ultimate catalyst for pain and brokenness, and it harms all our relationships, whether at work, home, or school. Every family has experienced the pain caused by sin, but have you ever wondered *why* sin hurts in the first place?

Sin *must* hurt because God designed a universe where every action has an equal and opposite reaction. If there were no consequences for sin, we would be less likely to change our behavior or strive for decency and godliness. However, though this statement is true, it distracts from the much more important reality that sin hurts because it's the natural consequence of stealing worship from God. Though the pain of consequences may motivate us to change our behavior, changing behavior for the purpose of avoiding consequences is just as self-centered as the original sin we committed. God deserves our obedience for Who He is, not so that we can avoid the pain of consequences. In a world created to thrive on righteousness, the presence of sin is devastating. Likewise, in a family meant to flourish in harmony, strife destroys peace.

How, then, can we avoid the pain brought about by sin? I wrote this book specifically to help you find the Cure for sin and the strife it produces in your home. First, however, we need to understand the Consequences of strife-creating sin in our families and the impact strife has on our lives. It may surprise you to discover that while the Consequences of sin are all bad, what God desires to do in our lives through these Consequences is good.

The ramifications for sin fall into two distinct categories:

- *Secondary Consequences* are the outcomes that occur when sin has been discovered and acted upon by a human agent. These consequences include being grounded, spanked, fired, arrested, and anything considered "punishment."

- *Primary Consequences,* on the other hand, occur *every* time someone sins. This is true even when the sin occurs only in the mind of the transgressor with no other human awareness. These primary consequences have three facets: Personal Hurt, Interpersonal Hurt, and Divine Hurt.

Personal Hurt

Personal hurt includes the physical suffering, mental anguish, and emotional pain one suffers from one's own sin. Spiritual destruction, however, is the greatest element of personal hurt. Every time we sin, our conscience becomes a little more seared, making it easier to sin again (I Timothy 4:2). This is why Ephesians 4:19 tells us that those who reject God's revealed truth "have become callous and have given themselves up to sensuality, greedy to practice every kind of impurity." Several other scriptures support this as well: Proverbs 26:27 says, "Whoever digs a pit will fall into it, and a stone will come back on him who starts it rolling," and Romans 1:18-32 outlines the horrific deterioration of continued, unconfessed sin. When we sin frequently, it weakens our spiritual "muscles" and moves us closer to destruction.

Interpersonal Hurt

Interpersonal hurt encompasses the physiological, mental, emotional, and spiritual consequences our sin has on others. Some believe these consequences only occur when the transgressor is caught in their iniquity, but even undetected sin has real consequences, not the least of which is undermining relationships. Proverbs 17:25 tells us, "A foolish son is a grief to his father and bitterness to her who bore him." No relationship can thrive in the soil of foolishness, deception, and rebellion.

Divine Hurt

Divine hurt is the very real consequence of our sin against God. Those lacking a relationship with God continually flaunt their rebellious will in His face, and for us who are born again, our sin strangles our prayers and drowns out the Holy Spirit's illumination in our lives. We displease God by stealing His glory through receiving to ourselves the worship due Him. Proverbs 15:9 says, "The way of the wicked is an abomination to the LORD, but he loves him who pursues righteousness."

Strife is one of Satan's most painful weapons used to batter our families, and this trifecta of hurt is woven into the very warp and woof of strife. To begin finding the Cure for strife, let's examine three specific ways strife scars every family member who's ever lived.

Strife Explodes without Warning

Do you remember our theme verse for this study? "The beginning of strife is like letting out water . . ." (Proverbs 17:14).

Like the deluge of a fire hydrant on a city street, when strife breaks out, it breaks out hard. A comical illustration of this is the first time I used a pressure sprayer to clean my porch. I didn't have anyone to teach me how it worked, but everything went fine until I noticed my leather sandals were also dirty and thought, "Hey, let me spray these off too!" When I was done, my sandals were clean but also gashed with long, crisscrossing slices deep in the leather.

Strife has the same effect—everyone gets hurt the moment it appears. Depending on the circumstances, there may be either physical, mental, or emotional pain, but there will always be spiritual pain along with it.

LifeWork Questions

1. Is there hurt and pain in your home due to strife?   Yes   No

2. Does the strife appear seemingly out of nowhere?   Yes   No

See how easy this LifeWork was! Whether a simple answer or a detailed study, taking the time to respond to the Lifework questions will help! (Isn't that why you're reading this book?) And it won't hurt . . . much.

Strife Separates Families

"A dishonest man spreads strife, and a whisperer separates close friends" (Proverbs 16:28).

Dishonesty between people always causes strife. The division dishonesty causes in a relationship may be veiled for a time, but it *will* manifest because you can't build a solid relationship on lies. Whether it's the liar's guilt seeping out through defensiveness or bitterness slowly influencing subtle rebellion, no one can have a healthy relationship with dishonesty present.

Although the passage above illustrates the division caused by lying, this separation principle encompasses all strife. Family members should be our closest friends, but strife doesn't discriminate; it deconstructs the tightest relationships. I cannot begin to enumerate the times I've observed friends "just messing around" who were at each other throats moments later. Strife decimates the home in the same way. Some might point out that sharing a painful experience knits people closer together. That only occurs, however, when they're both being attacked from the *outside*. When individuals attack each other, the experience only divides.

LifeWork Questions

When answering these questions, something to note is that it only takes one family member to cause consternation in the entire house. Identifying the *most* strained relationships will help pinpoint the epicenter of the strife. Look out for the *Most Common Denominator*—the person who has issues with everyone when no one else appears to have problems with each other. Remember that the Most Common Denominator won't always be one of the children—it may be a parent.

1. Is there relational carnage in your home because of strife?   Yes   No

2. Which relationships in your family are the most strained?

_____

_____

_____

_____

Strife Ruins Even the Most Enjoyable Times

"Better is a dry morsel with quiet than a house full of feasting with strife" (Proverbs 17:1).

No matter how wonderful the outing, how holy the holiday, how joyous the party, or how delicious the feast . . . if allowed, strife will ruin it. Often, it's the very activity we hoped would bring cheer that results in quarreling.

A clear illustration of this is the average Sunday morning. No God-loving family wakes up on the Lord's Day intent on tearing each other apart. Many families genuinely understand the significance and beauty of God's people assembling for corporate worship and are excited to fellowship with the Body of Christ. Yet, often before any teeth are brushed, an unnecessary fight breaks out in the home. It seems to explode in an extra-aggressive way on this particular day of the week. Voices are elevated, doors are slammed, and then the families try to reign in the arguing right as they pull into the church parking lot. Even the divine act of loving one another is prone to strife and discord.

LifeWork Questions

Consider these questions carefully because identifying specific activities the family *avoids* will first assist in recognizing who the chief strife Creators are and, second, help you understand the particular ways the strife Creators create strife. For example, when your children ask to play their game system, you hesitate because every time they play, strife explodes in the living room. You may notice that strife begins specifically when the eldest child loses to a younger sibling. This insight identifies who creates the strife as well as highlights the Cause.

1. Is it difficult to enjoy the people and events in your home because of strife?   Yes   No

2. What activities won't you even consider because you know they result in contention?

_____

_____

_____

_____

Strife Always Destroys

The inarguable fact is that strife will always destroy. It is fundamentally divisive and hurtful and detonates without warning. The closest relationships and the most enjoyable activities are potential feasts for strife's ravenous appetite. Then again, if we're being realistic, strife isn't a creature lurking in the shadows waiting to devour our family time. As we learned in the last chapter, strife arises from *people*.

Your LifeWork answers to this point should have revealed that strife isn't actually the real issue. The problem is the *people* who create the strife. Sin is the Cause, and strife is the Consequence, but sin comes from people. The good news is that God wants to use your family's strife for the good of the people in your home.

God Wants to Use Your Family Strife to Mature You

Strife is the result of sinful people doing sinful things, but that doesn't remove the fact that in the same way you hope to parent your children to maturity, God will use the strife in your life to mature you and conform you to the image of Christ.

Consider the words the apostle James wrote to the early Church,

> Count it all joy, my brothers, when you meet trials of various kinds, 3 for you know that the testing of your faith produces steadfastness. 4 And let steadfastness have its full effect, that you may be perfect and complete, lacking in nothing (James 1:2-4).

The phrase "trials of various kinds" includes the testing God allows into our lives as well as the temptations we face in our hearts. The strife in a home occurs when someone gives in to temptation and fails God's test. Now, you may ask, "Why does God allow us to be tested in the first place?" The answer lies within the passage. Verse 3 tells us that our tests are designed to produce an unwavering steadfastness in our faith. Like testing water quality or the purity of gold, these tests reveal the authenticity of our faith, and if we allow Him to refine us, they strengthen our trust in Him. It's interesting to note that the Greek word for "testing" (*dokimion*[5]) in James 1:3 means "that by which something is tried or proved, a test" and is only used in one other New Testament passage, I Peter 1:7. In that passage Peter begins with a beautiful summation of the gospel. Notice the astounding similarity between James 1:2-4 (above) and I Peter 1:6-9:

> In this you rejoice, though now for a little while, if necessary, you have been grieved by various trials, 7 so that the tested genuineness of your faith—more precious than gold that perishes though it is tested by fire—may be found to result in praise and glory and honor at the revelation of Jesus Christ. 8 Though you have not seen him, you love him. Though you do not now see him, you believe in him and rejoice with joy that is inexpressible and filled with glory, 9 obtaining the outcome of your faith, the salvation of your souls.

These scriptures show that when we are tested, God can divinely use the subsequent negative reaction of strife to purify our faith to the glory and honor of Jesus Christ! I must add, however, lest we get the wrong impression, that strife doesn't exist because God is testing your family. Strife exists

---

[5] G1383 – *dokimion* – Strong's Greek Lexicon

because one or more people have given in to temptation. To support this, James 1:13-15 goes on to say:

> Let no one say when he is tempted, "I am being tempted by God," for God cannot be tempted with evil, and he himself tempts no one. [14] But each person is tempted when he is lured and enticed by his own desire. [15] Then desire when it has conceived gives birth to sin, and sin when it is fully grown brings forth death.

God Has No Part in Temptation

The first thing that needs to be understood is that God doesn't entice anyone to sin. The second is that God cannot be tempted to sin. Though someone may try to persuade God to sin (as Satan did to Jesus in Matthew 4), God can't be enticed. Nothing in God desires evil. Sin is everything God isn't. If there were even a part of Him that was interested in sinning, He would cease to be God because God cannot desire, be enticed by, or be tempted to sin. People, on the other hand, are quite the opposite.

Man Has Every Part in Temptation

Temptation arises in people when our desires entice us to evil. Giving in to those desires leads to sin, which leads to death (Romans 6:23). Our sin is never anyone else's fault. Satan may tempt us, but we don't sin because of *him*. We don't yell at our kids because *they* broke a dish. You don't neglect your wife because *she* forgot to refill the gas or seemed uninterested in the events of our day. Our family, and even demonic forces, may be tempting us from the outside, but our choice to submit to their enticement is due to the disposition of our own hearts.

Let me provide an example of how this works between two people. God gives us choices and commands us to choose. This is the testing from God. Adam and Eve had a choice to obey God or eat the fruit (Genesis 2:16-17). Abraham had the option to obey God or refuse to sacrifice his son (Genesis 22:2). We have the choice to obey God or dishonor our spouses (Romans 12:10).

Picture a wife having to choose between what she wants and what her husband would like (she is being tested by God). Her sinful heart entices her to favor herself (her own temptation), so she chooses to disregard her husband's wishes and does what she wants. Strife ensues.

At this point, the strife may be entirely one-sided, but often it doesn't end there. Now, the husband has a choice—he can respond in patience, understanding, truth, and love (this is his divine test), or he can respond with selfishness and hostility (his own temptation). For the sake of this illustration, let's say he gives in to his own temptation (as so many of us do) and reacts in self-worship instead of being obedient to God for His glory. The strife has now become two-sided and will continue to escalate until one or preferably both discover the Cure for strife and submit to God.

Upon learning these truths many might ask, since God knows everything, why must our faith be tested? To answer this, I bring you back to what James 1:3-4 says:

> For you know that the testing of your faith produces steadfastness. 4 And let steadfastness have its full effect, that you may be perfect and complete, lacking in nothing."

The testing of our faith doesn't reveal anything to God; it *produces* something in us. According to this Scripture, the first thing testing should produce in us is steadfastness. This means when we're tested, we should grow in patience, endurance, perseverance, and consistency. Verse 4 also tells us that steadfastness produces maturity. Godly maturity signifies us being brought to His predestined end in our conformity to the image of Christ. This process is complete in that it touches every part of our being, so nothing inferior is left in us.

The second truth revealed in this scripture is that maturity produces blessing. As is true for most biblical promises, this one is conditional. Here, we see that *if* Christians remain steadfast, they *will* receive God's promised crown of life. The only other time the phrase "crown of life" is used in the New Testament is in Revelation 2:10 when Jesus tells the church in Smyrna:

> Do not fear what you are about to suffer. Behold, the devil is about to throw some of you into prison, that you may be tested, and for ten days you will have tribulation. Be faithful unto death, and I will give you the crown of life.

Once again, we see God's blessing as a byproduct of the correct response to testing and trials. This, however, is not merely a promise our Lord presented to the people in Smyrna. In Matthew, Jesus made a double-sided promise and command:

> "Blessed are you when others revile you and persecute you and utter all kinds of evil against you falsely on my account. 12 Rejoice and be glad, for your reward is great in heaven, for so they persecuted the prophets who were before you (Matthew 5:11-12).

To sum it all up, as uncomfortable as family strife is, as long as you are not the reason for the strife, God will use that discomfort to bring you to maturity and blessing. For this, we can rejoice and be glad while there is strife in our home. Of course, God still expects us to work with our families to reduce strife to His honor and glory, but the process is not accidental; it's a blessing.

Keep this in mind as we move on to the next chapter to investigate the Causes of strife. There is hope, no matter how bad the situation is.

LifeWork Assignment

Commit James 1:2-4 to memory:

> Count it all joy, my brothers, when you meet trials of various kinds, 3 for you know that the testing of your faith produces steadfastness. 4 And let steadfastness have its full effect, that you may be perfect and complete, lacking in nothing.

If you truly want God to use a time of trial to purify you, then consider also memorizing Psalm 119:9-11.

> How can a young man keep his way pure? By guarding it according to your word. 10 With my whole heart I seek you; let me not wander from your commandments! 11 I have stored up your word in my heart, that I might not sin against you.

Committing Scripture to memory is a vital part of maturity.

Closing Thoughts

To close this chapter on strife's Consequences, remember that any parent can stop a fight between their children, but wouldn't it be so much better to parent our children to peaceful maturity? Much like God does, we must use strife as a means to teach our children to resist the temptation to respond and escalate. To reduce the strife in our homes, we need to stop focusing on the conflict and start addressing the conflicted hearts involved.

Therefore, if maturing a heart is the goal, it is vitally important to understand *why* your strife Creators multiply strife. The next chapter will pull back the curtain of our souls to reveal the biblical Causes of strife that reside in every Creator of strife.

Part 3

The Causes of Strife

4
Deliberate Unbelief

You may have seen the heading on the previous page and wondered, "The Causes of strife? I thought the Causes were discussed in the first chapters. Aren't my dishonest, prideful spouse and my greedy, selfish children the problem?" Well, technically, those chapters pinpointed the types of sin that break through our dams and create strife. The goal of part three is to figure out *why* there's so much acidic, sinful water behind your family's dam walls in the first place.

When you understand the *spiritual nature of strife* within your family, the Cure will make far more sense. While the opening chapters dealt with the Creators of strife, this chapter and the next will deal with the specific spiritual Causes that exist *within* the Creators. We will also explore why some people store more toxic water in their dams than others.

Let's begin by imagining an aerial view of a dam; the cover of this book may help you form the image. Can you see the wall of self-control straining under the weight of all that sinfully erosive acidic water? Now, picture the beautiful countryside below the dam wall. What would happen if the dam ever collapsed? It would be pretty terrible.

This imagery reminds me of the 1978 *Superman* movie with Christopher Reeve. Using the best special effects of the day, the Creators showed us what it would look like for a dam to be destroyed by an earthquake and for a mountain of water to descend on a quiet town. Peter Jackson's *The Two Towers* had a similar scene where the ents drown the orc-infested Isengard by destroying a dam. But for our illustration, we've already seen the Consequences of strife, we're more interested in the *origin* of all that sinfully acidic water.

So, as you picture that massive dam, zoom out in your imagination. From here you should be able to see the entire lake of sin that fills our spiritual reservoirs. This lake represents our sinful hearts and strife-creating potential. But from where does all this acid come? How does it get into our lakes in the first place?

Let's imagine a massive pipeline on the backside of the lake dumping thousands of gallons of water into our reservoir every single day. This pipeline exists in everyone's life. It's the source of all sin; it's called the *sin nature.* Romans 5:12 tells us how this sinful nature originally entered our lives: "Therefore, just as sin came into the world through one man, and death through sin, and so death spread to all men because all sinned." Adam was the first man to sin, and as descendants of Adam, we all inherit his fallen, sinful nature. While we walk the Earth, it is a certainty we will contend with sin. It's woven through our very DNA. According to I John 1:8, we're liars if we suggest that we don't have any sin.

So, the logical question is, "If everyone has an equally gigantic aqueduct pouring sin-water into their reservoir, why don't we all have the same amount of poisonous acid behind our dam walls? Why don't we all cause the same amount of strife?" Part of the answer deals with the strength of our individual walls. The strength of our dam wall is based primarily on our self-control. However, the second part of the answer deals specifically with the *amount* of sin applying pressure to our self-control. The main difference between those who cause a lot of strife and those who cause very little has more to do with the Holy Spirit-empowered gift of sanctification.

So, in keeping with our metaphor, all believers who submit to God's rule in their lives are given access to a special control room near the mouth of the aqueduct. Those who enter the control room will see three levers. These levers have one purpose; they function like the handles on a faucet—they can decrease the water flow or increase it. Once we submit to the Holy Spirit's control in our lives, we realize that through the power of the Spirit we actually have a choice concerning the amount of sin that exists in our lives.

Let's imagine a best case scenario. Suppose all three levers were deactivated, and the pipeline were completely closed. The flow of water would cease entirely, meaning no more sinful acid would ever enter our lakes! Over time, the amount of sin-influence inside our lives would slowly diminish, and the amount of pressure on our self-control would decrease. Eventually, the potential of strife issuing from our lives would be nonexistent!

Unfortunately, on this side of Heaven, that can never happen. Anyone who tells you otherwise is sorely mistaken. We're incapable of *completely* eradicating sin in this life. Ultimately, that's God's job, and His Word says sin will be part of our earthly existence until He glorifies His followers in eternity (I John 3:2; Romans 8:29-30). However, even though it's impossible for this "faucet" to be turned off completely, Christians can drastically *reduce* the flow of sin to minimize its effect on our lives. This process requires the supernatural work of grace, but it is possible.

I'm going to continue explaining this supernatural process of sanctification using our pipeline illustration. Here's a very oversimplified picture of how this process works: when we activate the first lever, the gigantic pipeline closes a third of the way, decreasing the water flowing into your reservoir. The flow is reduced by another third when the second lever is engaged. Lastly, when the final lever is deactivated, the faucet closes *almost* all the way. Though sinful water will continue to pour into the reservoir, the flow is barely a trickle compared to the torrent it once was. Again, this illustration is deliberately oversimplified because the main goal of Part 3 is not to provide detailed instructions for overcoming sin in our lives, but instead to reveal the relationship between the Causes and the strife.

So, hypothetically, how would one actually close the pipeline? How can we reduce the flow of strife-causing sin as much as is humanly possible? The first observation is that the ability to close any of the three levers requires the power of the Holy Spirit. Nonbelievers have no hope of stemming the flow of sin pouring into their lives. I'm not suggesting, however, that all nonbelievers cause more strife than all followers of Christ. God's common grace is a merciful and beautiful gift He pours on all mankind. As discussed in an earlier chapter, common grace keeps all sinners from being as bad as they could be. It allows men, women, and children to live out a functional kind of righteousness even though they do so for selfish reasons.

The true difference arises when your family members submit to God's rule—because only then do they have access to the control room of their pipeline. With the assistance of the Spirit, closing the valve requires denial of our sinful flesh in three unique ways. The following New Testament passages beautifully illustrate precisely how to deactivate these levers. The first lever is the most important because all of the others can only close by first closing this initial valve.

1. We Must Deny Deliberate Unbelief

Romans 1:18-32 is a sad passage indeed. It chronicles the devastating fall of those who reject God's revealed Word. As we progress through the passage, I will comment on each portion so you can understand *why* God gives these people up. Let's first focus on two critical verses toward the end of the passage that reveal the danger of refusing to submit to God's authority:

> And since they did not see fit to acknowledge God, God gave them up to a debased mind to do what ought not to be done. [29] They were filled with all manner of unrighteousness, evil, covetousness, malice. They are full of envy, murder, **strife**, deceit, maliciousness. They are gossips. Romans 1:28-29 (my emphasis in bold).

Verse 28 demonstrates that willful disobedience to God generates strife. Keeping this in mind, let's look into the details of the first six verses:

> For the wrath of God is revealed from heaven against all ungodliness and unrighteousness of men, **who by their unrighteousness suppress the truth.** [19] For what can be known about God is plain to them, because God has shown it to them. [20] For his invisible attributes, namely, his eternal power and divine nature, have been clearly perceived, ever since the creation of the world, in the things that have been made. So they are without excuse. [21] For although they knew God, **they did not honor him as God or give thanks to him,** but **they became futile in their**

thinking, and **their foolish hearts were darkened.** 22 Claiming to be wise, **they became fools,** 23 and **exchanged the glory of the immortal God for images resembling mortal man and birds and animals and creeping things.**
Romans 1:18-23 (my emphasis in bold)

Take note, their sin is not merely ungodliness and unrighteousness. These unrighteous people *deliberately suppress* the truth. They know many things about God because He has shown them His truth, yet they *still* choose to dishonor Him. They also *consciously* exchange the worship of God for the worship of His creation. It's because of this rebellious mindset that God allows them to wallow in the cesspool they have chosen:

> Therefore **God gave them up** in the lusts of their hearts to impurity, to the dishonoring of their bodies among themselves, 25 because they exchanged the truth about God for a lie and worshiped and served the creature rather than the Creator, who is blessed forever! Amen.
> Romans 1:24-25 (my emphasis in bold)

Yet again, we see how people in this depraved group dishonor their bodies in service to a lie. It's also important to note that God allows these people to reject Him. He sets before all people life and death, He encourages all to choose life (Deuteronomy 30:19), He empowers His people to follow Him, and He allows others to reject His rule in their lives:

> For this reason **God gave them up** to dishonorable passions. For their women exchanged natural relations for those that are contrary to nature; 27 and the men likewise gave up natural relations with women and were consumed with passion for one another, men committing shameless acts with men and receiving in themselves the due penalty for their error.
> Romans 1:26-27 (my emphasis in bold)

The excerpt above shows the progression of sin: it starts with deliberately suppressing the truth and then devolves into shameless acts that carry a penalty. The following five verses underscore the inevitable trajectory of a life layered with sin and the resultant chaos when people refuse to acknowledge God:

> 28 And since they did not see fit to acknowledge God, **God gave them up** to a debased mind to do what ought not to be done. 29 They were filled with all manner of unrighteousness, evil, covetousness, malice. They are

full of envy, murder, strife, deceit, maliciousness. They are gossips, 30 slanderers, haters of God, insolent, haughty, boastful, inventors of evil, disobedient to parents, 31 foolish, faithless, heartless, ruthless. 32 **Though they know God's righteous decree that those who practice such things deserve to die, they not only do them but give approval to those who practice them.**
Romans 1:28-32 (my emphasis in bold)

Please reread verse 32: "Though they know God's righteous decree that those who practice such things deserve to die, **they not only do them but give approval to those who practice them.**"

Wow! It's vital for believers and unbelievers alike to recognize that sin is natural, immaturity is ignorance, but *disbelief is willful*.

The Merest Christianity podcast series taught us that *all sin is rooted in disbelief.* This takeaway is arguably the most important truth any Christian can learn. It deals with the most seminal part of our relationship with God. If you haven't yet heard this series, the sentence "all sin is rooted in disbelief" may seem difficult to accept at face value, but it's the truth nonetheless. If the lever of disbelief is *not* deactivated, the deluge of sin roaring into our lives causes the highest degree of destruction, leading to the most painful strife. Most Christians acknowledge that a sinner can deliberately choose to disbelieve God, or they can ignorantly disbelieve God. Still, it may be hard to imagine a *believer* intentionally disbelieving God's Word. Although you may think this impossible, I offer two additional observations:

The Merest Christianity

- There will be many in the last days who thought their salvation was assured, but who will find out they were never born again (Matthew 7:21-23).
- Every time we choose our way over God's, we're choosing not to love Him, and we're calling Him a liar—even if we're born again (John 14:15).

As sad as the first observation is, it must embolden us to help each of our family members know for sure they are children of God. If they don't submit to the Lord, strife will dominate their present *and* their eternal future. This reality is of such vital importance I've logged many hours studying the topic from Scripture. I present much of that study at TruthLoveParent.com

The Second Most Important Question

The Four Children

under the category *Evangelism Parenting*. If you're interested in learning how someone who believes they're saved may discover they don't truly have a relationship with God, you should listen to the following episodes: *The Second Most Important Question to Ask Your Children*, and *The Four Children* series. The information presented in these episodes suggests that a professing Christian may not believe God because he's mistaken concerning his salvation.

Now let's consider the second observation that every time anyone chooses their way over God's, they're choosing not to love Him, and they're calling Him a liar—even if they're born again. As previously mentioned, the biblical concept of a genuine Christian not loving God with all his heart, soul, and mind is difficult for many Christians to absorb. We learn from I John 4:19 that Christians have the love of God in them, and we learn from I Corinthians 13 that love is never-ending. So, how can it be said that a Christian does not love God? Ken Collier of The Wilds[6] says, "Just two choices on the shelf, pleasing God or pleasing self." Love is a choice to want and work toward God's best interest for the one loved. Not loving God is a choice to set your desire above His glory. When I selfishly love myself more than God, I've set myself against Him.

In John 14:15, Jesus says, "If you love me, you will keep my commandments." The obvious counterpoint to this declaration is that if you don't obey Him, you don't love Him. Most of the time, I sin without thinking; I *feel* my way into stupid decisions. Although my emotions usually draw me into sin, I can be honest enough to admit I've often—in a state of rebellion—*deliberately* chosen to do what I knew was wrong. Though it may sound suspect to suggest a "believer" doesn't "believe" God, when we define the words biblically, we can easily see that a genuinely born-again individual can

---

[6] "The Wilds." n.d. The Wilds. https://wilds.org/.

still practically choose to ignore God's commands, believing his own sinful way is best.

An unfortunate example of this disbelief in my own life is painfully illustrated in the "The Mushroom Wars." When I used to cook with mushrooms, I never washed them. Sure, if there were a large chunk of dirt, I wiped it off, but—for the most part—unwashed mushrooms never bothered me. However, they did bother my wife.

Now, I *know* the Bible says that we need to live with our wives according to knowledge, and I *know* what it is to love my wife, but my refusal to wash the mushrooms grew from the fact that I didn't *believe* I needed to do that in order to love my wife. I believed she was being ridiculous, and I believed she was the one who needed to change. It was a belief so strong that I would ignore her requests, I even sometimes tried to give her the impression I washed the mushrooms without doing it, and quite often my words were cutting and strife-filled . . . all because in those moments I didn't believe I was doing anything wrong. I was choosing my own way over God's, I wasn't loving Him (or my wife), and I was calling Him a liar . . . even though I was a Christian.

Okay, let's circle back to the bottom line: every time we consciously choose to disbelieve and/or disobey, whether born again or not, we slam so much toxic, sinful acid against our dam of self-control that it's almost impossible to contain it. When we consciously or subconsciously allow the lever of deliberate unbelief to remain active, we can be confident that sin will regularly flow into and through our lives. However, even if we firmly close the lever of willful unbelief, the sin-nature aqueduct is still two-thirds open. Therefore, we must learn how to close the second and third levers to further stem the flow as much as possible.

The good news is there is a tried and true method to gain access to these levers and deactivate them. Keep reading; you'll love how simple it is.

LifeWork Question

Think carefully and honestly: have you, your spouse, or your children been guilty of deliberately disregarding God's truth? If so, is it because you lack genuine spiritual life or because you, like all of us, foolishly choose to love your own way? Knowing the difference will change how you grow personally, parent your children[7], and disciple others.

---

[7] Figuring out if their rejection grows from a dead heart or a conflicted (but regenerated) heart will help you parent their specific needs better.

5
Immaturity & Fleshly Living

I love the way Paul calls people out. No beating about the bush—this confident apostle just speaks the simple truth. He tells the Corinthian believers they are, in a spiritual sense, *utterly* immature:

> But I, brothers, could not address you as spiritual people, but as people of the flesh, as infants in Christ. ² I fed you with milk, not solid food, for you were not ready for it. And even now you are not yet ready, ³ for you are still of the flesh. For while there is jealousy and **strife** among you, are you not of the flesh and behaving only in a human way?
> I Corinthians 3:1-3—my emphasis in bold

Notice that Paul goes on to explain how their immaturity restricts their spiritual growth. His illustration aptly describes their spiritual immaturity—which is the second lever in the control room of the metaphorical pipeline pouring sinful acid into our lives. This chapter reveals how we recognize the second and third levers and how deactivating these levers drastically decreases the volume of sin being pumped into our lives. Let's dive right in.

We're all less spiritually mature than we should be, so to some degree, we're *all* immature. This immaturity is the point of testing we discussed in the third chapter; God is helping us become *more* steadfast and *mature*. The immaturity on which we're focusing here is *consistent* and *systemic* immaturity. I think a prior observation can provide contextual meaning for our understanding of "immaturity" in this chapter: "Sin is natural, *immaturity is ignorance*, disbelief is willful."

For people to mature, they must cycle through three stages known as the Circle of Learning. The first step in this Circle is the acquisition of *knowledge*, which is a direct attack on ignorance. This step must be taken in order to progress to the second and third stages, which are *understanding* and *wisdom*.

The Circle of Learning

2. We Must Deny Spiritual Immaturity

I established in the previous chapter that—from a biblical perspective—spiritual immaturity is always the result of disbelief. Whether deliberate or accidental, rejecting God's truth parades our ignorance, and ignorance is

anything but bliss because it invites four dire consequences into our lives. Immature people:
1. sin more frequently
2. are ignorant of their actual struggles
3. believe they're better than they really are
4. require more help to change

Let's assess the consequences of spiritual immaturity in more detail:

1. **We all sin, but immature people sin more frequently**.

When did you last see a room of toddlers playing in complete harmony? It seldom happens given their immaturity. A pastor friend of mine used to say, "We'll never be sinless this side of Heaven, but we should sin less and less." That's one way of understanding II Corinthians 3:18, "And we all, with unveiled face, beholding the glory of the Lord, are being transformed into the same image from one degree of glory to another. For this comes from the Lord who is the Spirit."

Essentially, this Scripture explains that the more we learn and believe the truth of the Bible, the more we reflect God's glory. While we are being "transformed into the same image," we are increasing the degree of our maturity, gaining understanding and wisdom in the process.

Your family will have immaturity among its members as long as they are not focused on God and are, therefore, ignorant of His truth.

2. **Immature people are ignorant of their actual struggles**.

In I Timothy 1:13, Paul tells Timothy, "Formerly I was a blasphemer, persecutor, and insolent opponent. But I received mercy because I had acted ignorantly in unbelief." Paul is describing his life before conversion, but the effects of the sin nature are easily applied to immature believers as well, who act ignorantly due to their immaturity. If someone claims to be a Christian and willfully chooses to live in sin, Jesus commands us to remove him from the fellowship of the saints and treat him as an unbeliever (Matthew 18:15-17).

The apostle John presents a similar concept regarding willful sin:

> "If we say we have no sin, we deceive ourselves, and the truth is not in us. [9] If we confess our sins, he is faithful and just to forgive us our sins and to cleanse us from all unrighteousness. [10] If we say we have not sinned, we make him a liar, and his word is not in us."
> I John 1:8-10

When confronted by biblical truth, a mature believer will eventually submit. He'll learn from the experience, seek to understand it, and wisely respond—ultimately revealing further growth.

There will be strife in your family if those who are immature continue to be ignorant of their sin.

3. **Immature people believe they're better than they really are**.

The flip side of not realizing you're wrong is pridefully assuming you're right. It's akin to a child who decides to stick a paper clip into an electrical socket despite being warned of the dangers. By thinking we know better than God how we should live, we demonstrate to the more mature how spiritually infantile we genuinely are. Twice in Proverbs (14:12 and 16:25), we read, "There is a way that seems right to a man, but its end is the way to death."

Those who make destructive choices while believing they're good choices are immature and will cause strife in your family.

4. **Immature people require more help to change**.

The metaphor Paul uses in I Corinthians 3 is powerful and humbling. He tells the Corinthians that due to their spiritual immaturity, they have only been able to survive on milk rather than graduating to solid food. Even as Paul wrote, he knew they could still not handle spiritual meat because of their lack of spiritual growth.

Immature people sin more often and don't recognize the problem they have. Instead, they think they're doing well, and this skewed mindset requires a more focused investment to rectify.

The reality is that the Flesh is our inescapable, natural burden while we live on this Earth, making it easy to give in to fleshly temptation, which ultimately breeds strife. The truth, however, is that persistent immaturity is *unnatural*. God created every living thing in this universe to grow and change. Beings who do not mature go against the created order. This simple truth is why my children often hear me say, "If you're not growing, you're dead." It makes no sense for someone with spiritual life to remain ignorant of their sin and God's remedy.

Unnatural immaturity will always multiply the ease of sin and the consequential destruction strife brings.

LifeWork Question

Immature people cause more strife due to the frequency of their sins. But even though they cause so much strife, they often don't recognize the chaos surrounding them as strife. On the other hand, when they are aware of the strife, they often don't see themselves as the problem—they don't realize it is a result of *their* words or actions.

Are you spiritually immature?

Think carefully about your answer. Instead of automatically assuming you're not immature, use the above criteria to assess your accurate level of spiritual maturity.

Please ask your spouse or parent to critique you on this one. If their answer exposes anger or pride in you, be thankful God is revealing your immaturity and providing a way to grow away from spiritual ignorance and strengthen your faith.

Let's review our understanding of this metaphor in which we're "closing the aqueduct" of our sin nature.

First, this over-simplified metaphor is designed to help us see the three main Causes of sin in your family.

Second, shutting off the unbelief lever stops the flow of deliberate unbelief. When we close this portion of the flow, we can avoid significant strife—which is impossible for unbelievers. Also, until we close the flow of deliberate unbelief, we'll never be able to deactivate the other two toggles.

Third, as we disengage the immaturity lever, we'll see—year-over-year—the consistency of sin decrease and the amount of strife grandly and gloriously lessen.

Finally, as we toggle the third lever, we'll cease to be known as strife Creators. Therefore, let's consider what it takes to further stem the flow of sin in our lives.

3. We Must Deny Fleshly Living
Paul makes a distinction between two lifestyle choices: "works of the flesh" and "fruit of the Spirit."

> Now the **works of the flesh** are evident: sexual immorality, impurity, sensuality, 20 idolatry, sorcery, enmity, *strife*, jealousy, fits of anger, rivalries, dissensions, divisions, 21 envy, drunkenness, orgies . . . 22 But the **fruit of the Spirit** is love, joy, peace, patience, kindness, goodness, faithfulness, 23 gentleness, self-control.
> Galatians 5:19-23—my emphasis in bold

The "works of the flesh" and the "fruit of the Spirit" refer to the natural consequences of our spiritual choices. The "works of the flesh" illustrate well the natural results of people who live fleshly lives, as does the list of natural consequences relevant to those who bear the "fruit of the Spirit."

What does "the flesh" mean in this context? The word "flesh" often contrasts with the human spirit or the Holy Spirit. Your soul (your whole being) consists of two elements: your body and your spirit. Our current bodies are temporal, but our spirits are eternal—yet both carry the taint of sin passed down from Adam. Despite this fact, biblical writers under the inspiration of the Holy Spirit frequently distinguish between sinful (fleshly) living and righteous (spiritual) living. So, when God talks about our flesh, He is often referring to the fallen, sinful nature inherent in all humans (except Christ). This sinful nature is our natural predisposition.

In Matthew 26:41, Jesus drew a contrast between the flesh and the spirit when He told His disciples, "The spirit indeed is willing, but the flesh is weak." Jesus explained this contrast to Nicodemus in more detail: "Truly, truly, I say to you, unless one is born of water and the Spirit, he cannot enter the kingdom of God. 6 That which is born of the flesh is flesh, and that which is born of the Spirit is spirit" (John 3:5-6). Every time we fill our reservoirs with anger, greed, pride, hate, and foolishness, the Bible references this lifestyle choice as "living in the flesh." This inherently sinful nature of the flesh explodes through our self-control, creating strife in our lives and families.

This fleshly living is also just as much a problem in believers as it is in unbelievers. The difference is that unbelievers are in bondage to the flesh, whereas followers of Christ are enslaved to God. The unsaved person can't help but worship himself, while the Christian *chooses* to reject God and temporarily resubmit himself to his old master. I suppose this makes the fleshly sin of a Christian that much more abhorrent.

Romans exemplifies how we should be living now that we are free from bondage to the flesh:

> There is therefore now no condemnation for those who are in Christ Jesus. 2 For the law of the **Spirit** of life has set you free in Christ Jesus from the law of sin and death. 3 For God has done what the law,

weakened by the **flesh**, could not do. By sending his own Son in the likeness of sinful **flesh** and for sin, he condemned sin in the **flesh**, 4 in order that the righteous requirement of the law might be fulfilled in us, who walk not according to the **flesh** but according to the **Spirit**. 5 For those who live according to the **flesh** set their minds on the things of the **flesh**, but those who live according to the **Spirit** set their minds on the things of the Spirit. 6 For to set the mind on the **flesh** is death, but to set the mind on the **Spirit** is life and peace. 7 For the mind that is set on the **flesh** is hostile to God, for it does not submit to God's law; indeed, it cannot. 8 Those who are in the **flesh** cannot please God. 9 You, however, are not in the **flesh** but in the **Spirit**, if in fact the **Spirit** of God dwells in you. Anyone who does not have the **Spirit** of Christ does not belong to him. 10 But if Christ is in you, although the body is dead because of sin, the **Spirit** is life because of righteousness. 11 If the **Spirit** of him who raised Jesus from the dead dwells in you, he who raised Christ Jesus from the dead will also give life to your mortal bodies through his **Spirit** who dwells in you. 12 So then, brothers, we are debtors, not to the **flesh**, to live according to the **flesh**. 13 For if you live according to the **flesh** you will die, but if by the **Spirit** you put to death the deeds of the body, you will live. 14 For all who are led by the **Spirit** of God are sons of God. 15 For you did not receive the **spirit** of slavery to fall back into fear, but you have received the **Spirit** of adoption as sons, by whom we cry, "Abba! Father!" 16 The Spirit himself bears witness with our **spirit** that we are children of God, 17 and if children, then heirs—heirs of God and fellow heirs with Christ, provided we suffer with him in order that we may also be glorified with him.
Romans 8:1-17—my emphasis in bold

Yet, even though we can become children of God, justification doesn't simply eradicate the flesh—it *positionally* adds us to the Spirit. It's through sanctification that we slowly remove the flesh's power over us, yet only when we're glorified will we be completely free from the flesh. That's why Paul could transparently expose his struggle with the flesh:

For we know that the law is spiritual, but I am of the **flesh**, sold under sin. 15 For I do not understand my own actions. For I do not do what I want, but I do the very thing I hate. 16 Now if I do what I do not want, I agree with the law, that it is good. 17 So now it is no longer I who do it, but sin that dwells within me. 18 For I know that nothing good dwells in me, that is, in my **flesh**. For I have the desire to do what is right, but not the ability to carry it out. 19 For I do not do the good I want, but the evil I do not want is what I keep on doing. 20 Now if I do what I do not want, it is no longer I who do it, but sin that dwells within me. 21 So I find it to be

a law that when I want to do right, evil lies close at hand. 22 For I delight in the law of God, in my inner being, 23 but I see in my members another law waging war against the law of my mind and making me captive to the law of sin that dwells in my members. 24 Wretched man that I am! Who will deliver me from this body of death?
Romans 7:14-24—my emphasis in bold

I believe we all resonate with this passage because the apostle Paul, under the inspiration of the Holy Spirit, perfectly describes those times when confronted by a test from God—we choose to submit to sin and suffer the warring and strife that comes from fleshly living.

Finally, Titus puts into excellent perspective the importance of denying fleshly living:

For the grace of God has appeared, bringing salvation to all people, 12 instructing us to **deny ungodliness and worldly desires** and to live sensibly, righteously, and in a godly manner in the present age, 13 looking for the blessed hope and the appearing of the glory of our great God and Savior, Christ Jesus, 14 who gave Himself for us to redeem us from every lawless deed, and to purify for Himself a people for His own possession, eager for good deeds.
Titus 2:11-14, NASB—my emphasis in bold

As we begin to deny fleshly living, our self-control increases. Denying the flesh requires us to first flip the switch from "unbelief" to "belief" in God. Then, using our increasing knowledge and understanding, we must toggle the second switch away from spiritual immaturity—which enables us to throw the final switch, as we actively put away fleshly living in exchange for righteous living.

Interestingly, the English Standard Version translation specifically mentions "self-control" in verse 12: ". . . training us to renounce ungodliness and worldly passions, and **to live self-controlled, upright, and godly lives** in the present age . . ." (my emphasis in bold).

Now, let's consider one final point concerning our sinful nature. As previously mentioned, the final switch is powerless to close the aqueduct completely, which allows sinful water to continue pouring into our lives. We'll never be free of it this side of eternity; only Jesus Himself has the power necessary to engage that final lever entirely once and for all! Yes, by the power of God, by trusting Him, learning about Him, and putting what we've learned into practice, we can drastically affect the amount of sin manifested in our lives, but there will always be a remnant.

Lord, quickly come!

This remnant is why we have to expect there will always be at least a trickle of acid dripping into our reservoir . . . but we don't have to like it. The good news is when all three levers are closed as tightly as they can be, and the Holy Spirit strengthens your dam of self-control, you will no longer be the leading Creator of strife in your family—despite the persisting sin in your life. Additionally, the strife that does result from your sin will pale in comparison and be much easier to address.

LifeWork Project

What forms of fleshly living exist in your household? Galatians 5:19-21 is a fantastic starting point for answering this question. If necessary, do a quick study to see what each word means. It may be easy to dismiss the existence of "orgies" or "sorcery" in your family's life, but understanding what Paul meant by those words may help you see your family in a new light.

_____

_____

_____

Relationships among the Three Levers

Before closing this chapter and diving into the *Cure* for family strife, we need to see the relationships among the three levers. We have:

1. deliberate unbelief,
2. ignorant immaturity, and
3. natural fleshliness.

Unbelief will always produce spiritual immaturity and fleshly living. That connection is solid and sure. Fleshly living, although always a product of unbelief (all sin is), is not always a result of *intentional* unbelief. The similarity is unbelief, but spiritual maturity is the difference. This spiritual maturity is why a wise, righteous woman will continue to experience the results of the flesh until the day God calls her home. Her fleshly living, however, is not necessarily the result of conscious, defiant unbelief and rampant immaturity.

In the same way that one could say all Rottweilers are dogs, but not all dogs are Rottweilers, all conscious rebellion will produce fleshly living. Still, not all fleshly living is a result of *deliberate* rebellion.

So, what's the application?

We've already discussed how turning off the second and third levers is only possible if the first is already engaged, but which of these levers is the most difficult to close? Deciding to stop rejecting the Bible's truth is a hard one. It takes an act of God to even consider it. Yet, with His help, you can do it, and once the lever finally starts to move, it moves well.

The second lever is moved by increased knowledge which leads to understanding and wisdom. As we learn more about God and, by the power of the Holy Spirit, comprehend His instructions and put them to use, the lever of spiritual immaturity slides closed over the course of our lives.

The third lever, however, the one that can't be fully closed on this side of Heaven—that nagging sin nature that rears its ugly head despite the learning and growing we've experienced throughout our whole lives—is quite possibly the most challenging lever to address. It requires just as much Holy Spirit power and guidance as the other levers, but it's an arduous and seemingly fruitless work because the flesh will always be with us.

Why would I make this observation here at the end of the chapter?

It's easy to understand how rebellious, spiritually immature children can cause strife, but we must accept that although we are committed and—perhaps—more spiritually mature than our kids, we too can cause strife . . . and often do. Sure, it may not be as excessive and overpowering, but it's still there.

This reality means that we must remain ever-vigilant. There's no guarantee parents will *never* cause strife just because we're older and have experienced salvation for longer. The flesh will always be with us. Therefore, we—just like our children—need God's cure for family strife.

Our sinful nature, our ignorance resulting in immaturity, and our deliberate rebellion are the Causes that fill the Creators with the strife that invites the Consequences. So, what's the Cure?

An ancient king whose daily struggles far outweighed the strife in our families recorded the blueprint for our success. The next chapter will explain the hope this king placed in his God, his Rock, in whom he took refuge.

Part 4

The Cure for Strife

6
Trust the Truth & Submit to the Spirit

Okay, this is the moment for which we've all been waiting! How do we quit the strife? How do we stop the conflict for good? How do we close our sin pipelines and reduce the flow of iniquity pouring into our acidic lakes? What's the Cure?

The answer is revealed through a mighty warrior-king who faced untold life-and-death challenges, emerged victorious, and then illustrated his strategy in detail. This king of renown forged a path we can all follow, and by the close of this chapter, you will have a much greater understanding of how to cure the strife that infects your family.

To get started, the focus of this chapter and the next are the general principles that apply to all families. Both chapters will deal with understanding and implementing the general spiritual principles that cure strife in the home. Evermind Ministries has other resources investigating the specific needs of the nine strife-creating individuals discussed in chapters one and two. If you skimmed through those chapters, please re-read them carefully. Remember, it's desperately important to identify the strife Creators in your house. Start by uncovering the strife-creating character issues in your own life and then do the same for your family members. That information will make it much easier to address your family's unique situation.

"But, Aaron, you don't know my family!" you might say. "It's like the coliseum at my house. It's impossible for the children to have a civil conversation, and the tension is so high I feel like my spouse is constantly on the defensive. When I try to address it, things only get worse. I know precisely who the trouble-makers are, but how can I hope to change anything now?"

You're right, my friend. It would help if you had some hope.

The Possibility of Peace

First, it is imperative you start by simply believing that your family *can* be at peace; strife does not have to rule. The Bible is a message of eternal hope. Only Christ can offer true hope—believing this is the core of genuine salvation. Through Christ alone, you will find hope for your family's struggles. You must understand, however, that it's not about whether or not your family can change. *It's about God and His glory.*

Before we continue, let's find some hope in Psalm 18. The introduction to the Psalm tells us King David wrote it as a prayer to God after He had delivered David from His enemies, and its opening line sets the tone perfectly:

> I love you, O Lord, my strength. ² The Lord is my rock and my fortress and my deliverer, my God, my rock, in whom I take refuge, my shield, and the horn of my salvation, my stronghold. ³ I call upon the Lord, who is worthy to be praised, and I am saved from my enemies.
> Psalm 18:1-3

Having set the tone, David goes on to explain the severity of his problem. In just three verses, he uses the word "death" twice, speaks of being terrified and surrounded, and describes snares, distress, and torrents of ungodliness. I don't know your specific family issues, but Scripture illustrates David's persecution as vastly overshadowing the daily strife most of us encounter:

> The cords of death encompassed me; the torrents of destruction assailed me; ⁵ the cords of Sheol entangled me; the snares of death confronted me. ⁶ In my distress I called upon the Lord; to my God I cried for help. From his temple he heard my voice, and my cry to him reached his ears.
> Psalm 18:4-6

David reveals his top-secret tactic for meeting the onslaught of death and ungodliness in verse 6: "In my distress I called upon the Lord; to my God I cried for help." Do you daily present your strife Creators before the Lord? Are you beseeching Him on behalf of your family? I assure you He's waiting. He desperately wants to intercede but will not force His Cure upon us.

In the same way we had to approach Him for salvation, He wants us to cast all our cares on Him. The Lord promises to bear these weighty cares for us but will not forcibly take them from us. We must do the casting. When we do, we can say as David did in the second half of verse 6, "From his temple he heard my voice, and my cry to him reached his ears."

What happens next is a detailed description of how God came on the scene and dealt with the enemy. It would help if you took the time to read verses 7 through 15 for yourself. It uses beautiful imagery to help us glimpse the majesty and power of our rescuing God. Verses 16 through 19 then explain how God not only confronted the wicked but also rescued David by removing him from danger:

> He sent from on high, he took me; he drew me out of many waters. ¹⁷ He rescued me from my strong enemy and from those who hated me, for they were too mighty for me. ¹⁸ They confronted me in the day of my calamity, but the Lord was my support. 19 He brought me out into a broad place; he rescued me, because he delighted in me.
> Psalm 18:16-19

I must make an essential observation before we continue. I do not suggest you see your family as the "enemy" identified in verse 17. You and your family are on the same side. Sin is the enemy that causes strife. Ephesians 6:12 teaches us, "We do not wrestle against flesh and blood, but against the rulers, against the authorities, against the cosmic powers over this present darkness, against the spiritual forces of evil in the heavenly places."

So, what's the point of studying Psalm 18? God desires to protect us from our spiritual enemies like He protected David from his physical enemies. This Fatherly care He shows is why Ephesians 6 introduces the spiritual armor God has provided to protect us from the onslaught of our diabolical foe.

Are you encouraged yet?

Do you see how God stands ready with *everything you need* to wage spiritual warfare on the strife in your home? I hope you do see it, and I hope you are encouraged. Still, you may be feeling like you've called out to God over and over, but the Earth hasn't shaken, He hasn't arrived "swiftly on the wings of the wind" (Psalm 18:10), and He certainly didn't send "hailstones and coals of fire" (Psalm 18:12).

Thankfully, there's still more to learn in Psalm 18. In the same way that Ephesians 6 teaches us we can only overcome our spiritual enemies by putting on the character of God, David reveals God's salvation did not occur just because he asked. Consider verses 20 through 24:

> The Lord dealt with me according to my righteousness; according to the cleanness of my hands he rewarded me. 21 For I have kept the ways of the Lord, and have not wickedly departed from my God. 22 For all his rules were before me, and his statutes I did not put away from me. 23 I was blameless before him, and I kept myself from my guilt. 24 So the Lord has rewarded me according to my righteousness, according to the cleanness of my hands in his sight.
> Psalm 18:20-24

Do these verses describe you?

It's important to remember how many of God's promises are conditional. For example, we all love Romans 8:28 because it promises that all things will work together for good . . . but that's only half the promise. The condition of this promise is that things only work together for good *for those who love God and work toward His purposes*. Likewise, we cannot expect to be saved from our spiritual enemies when we're acting exactly like them!

Verses 29 through 50 of Psalm 18 read like a superhero movie. Verse 29 says, "For by you I can run against a troop, and by my God I can leap over a wall." I strongly encourage you to read how David describes the empowering grace of God through his ordeal. Be inspired that when you love the Lord and work biblically to stem the flow of strife in your home, God will equip you to overcome your real enemies: Satan, the World, and the Flesh.

In verse 43, we read, "You delivered me from strife with the people." David spent the entire Psalm praising God for being his rock and providing illustrations of the Lord's protection. Although this verse isn't technically a direct promise from God to you, it primarily reveals two miraculous truths:

1. God is the only One Who can shield us from strife.
2. Our sole responsibility is to love the Lord and serve Him in righteousness.

God hasn't tasked you with changing your spouse or children, but He commands that you submit to Him.

Now that our hope is founded securely in God, what steps can you take to cure the strife in your home? It all starts with you. Address yourself first, and then the Lord can use you to help heal your family.

The Cure for Strife

Some of you may feel you cannot begin to imagine how your little terrorist will ever be able to accomplish any of what follows. Remember, our hope is *not* in ourselves or our families. **Our hope is in God!** Psalm 71 proclaims: "For you, O Lord, are my hope, my trust, O Lord, from my youth" (Psalm 71:5). Jesus also teaches that "with man this is impossible, but with God all things are possible" (Matthew 19:26).

Some may think my description of the Cure for family strife is too easy— like the claim of a snake oil salesman who says, "This little bottle will cure all that ails ya!" Remember, though, God doesn't waste words. He gives us everything we need for life and godliness (II Peter 1:3), He never lies (Titus 1:2), and the Cure I present isn't my Cure at all . . . it comes directly from Scripture.

Even so, others might say, "Aaron, we've already tried what the Bible says, but it didn't work." This response is probably the most dangerous of all. Be careful. In I Corinthians 3:18, Paul says, "Let no one deceive himself. If anyone among you thinks that he is wise in this age, let him become a fool that he may become wise."

I teach martial arts and have had many opportunities to teach tiny children to break one inch pine boards with their bare hands. I start by teaching them the proper technique. The science is sound, and the method is proven, but I still have to warn the student when they attempt to break their first board. I say, "If the board doesn't break, it's not because 'you can't do it' or 'it's too hard' or 'your teacher didn't teach you correctly.' If the board doesn't break, you didn't follow the instructions. If the board doesn't break, you need to correct your technique." Sometimes, we parents think we're "wiser than God" by believing we kept His Word to a T—even though we didn't receive the outcome we thought He promised us. In those circumstances, I would caution you to reevaluate. If God didn't keep His promise, it wasn't because He dropped the ball. Perhaps we didn't obey as fully as we should have. Maybe we misunderstood His promise? Either way, the responsibility falls on us, not God.

A Self-Focus Creates Strife

There's one more crucial foundation stone to remember before we unveil the Cure for strife. At the end of chapter 2, I made the observation that parenting, discipleship, and counseling are experiences that either create strife or introduce peace. There is no middle ground. I asked us to consider that if how you relate to the people in your life flows from *who you are and what you want* to accomplish, then your relational approach is self-focused and self-motivated. In those cases, I presented the following unavoidable list:

1. You're addicted to your own desires.
2. You're not loving God because you're not obeying God.
3. You're not loving the people in your life because you're not relating to them in the best way you can.
4. You're desperately wanting your own way.
5. You're being dishonest with the people in your life about how you're meant to live your lives.
6. You're likely to become easily angered when you don't get the results you desire.
7. All this ultimately flows from being a prideful, arrogant individual who chooses to relate to the people in your life however you want to, despite what God says.
8. Biblically speaking, this prideful arrogance makes you a fool.

Please do not pursue God's Cure for your own peace and well-being! This is not about you and the strife in your home, it has to be about God and the glory He deserves.

A God-Focus Creates Peace

When you humbly submit to God's expectations for your life, you're being wise, and you're creating an atmosphere for peace to thrive.

1. If you're passionate about how God wants you to relate to the people in your life,

2. If you're giving the Lord the love due to Him by obeying His expectations for your relationships,
3. If you're loving everyone by relating to them in the best way you possibly can—better than you could ever muster through your own strength,
4. If you do this because you're zealous for God's way,
5. If you're honest with everyone about how God wants you and them to live,
6. And if you don't become easily angered because it's not about you . . .

. . . then strife will never flow from your life.

    Now, this is not to say that people will always love, admire, and submit to you if you're a humble Christ-follower. It's very possible your humility may be the thing they hate the most, but even though your family or friends may hate God's will and cause strife because of *their* life choices, the strife will not be due to *your* choices. Your dam wall will not be breaking. Your words will be God's words of peace.

    Our parenting and "spousing" and "friending" will either produce strife or peace, and we're fools if we think we can fix strife by introducing more strife. Fighting fire with fire does not work when we're talking about family contention. Your focus must be on good discipleship. I mention this because, quite often, parents are only really interested in "fixing" or "changing" their kids or "stopping" their children's bad behavior. The same is true of how we interact with our spouses. Those individuals who meet strife with strife are impotent to address the strife-causing issues in their family because they're reinforcing the negative cycle. How we interact with the people we love will produce either strife or peace, and it all starts with us trusting that God's way is best.

    As you dive into the next section, consider your own life first. Since you clearly desire to reduce the strife in your home, make sure your motivation and your methods are founded on Who God is and what He deserves. Lead your family in the right direction, the right way, and for the right reasons. Only then will you access His power to accomplish His goals for your family.

    This is why the LifeWork for the following four points all starts with you carefully considering your own heart before addressing your family.

    Having established these fundamental truths, here is the four-step Cure for the strife in your home:

1. Trust
2. Submit
3. Grow
4. Quit

1. Trust the Truth

If you ever participated in Truth.Love.Parent.'s *Merest Christianity* study, you know the most seminal facet of our humanity is our faith. Faith is the choice to accept something as true regardless of other factors. Simply put, faith is trust. When you tell me your family will be at our Friday Game Night, and I trust you will be there, I'm putting my faith in you. Trust is where true change always starts. If I don't trust God or His Word, I will not submit to either. If, however, I trust that God's way is best, I will obey His commands, receive His empowerment, and experience His blessing.

The Merest Christianity

A few chapters ago we learned that "an arrogant man stirs up strife, But he who trusts in the Lord will prosper" (Proverbs 28:25). Notice how this exquisite Hebrew poetry reveals that trust *requires* humility. The first part of the proverb explains that arrogance causes strife, and the second half presents the converse—whereas arrogant people do and say sinful things that produce strife, the humble man trusts in the Lord. This verse, by necessity, assumes the humble man obeys the Lord and is, therefore, not creating strife. When humble men, women, and children fully trust God, He causes them to prosper.

As I mentioned earlier, we must understand God's promises *the way He intends them*. God is not promising to increase my tangible wealth, heal my maladies, or stop my kids from rebelling. God's promises for His New Testament saints involve *internal* promises of spiritual strength, joy, peace, contentment, conformity to the character of Christ, and so much more—but it all revolves around *spiritual* blessing.

Consider again our discussion concerning Romans 1. In verse 21, we learn that *those who do not trust God* become futile in their thinking, and their hearts are darkened. Verse 29 reveals that "they were filled with all manner of unrighteousness, evil, covetousness, malice. They are full of envy, murder, strife, deceit, maliciousness. They are gossips." For better or worse, what we trust affects who we are. If I trust myself over God, I will live unrighteously, but when I trust God, the consequences result in my personal holiness.

LifeWork for You

"Choose this day whom you will serve . . . But as for me and my house, we will serve the Lord" (Joshua 24:15). You must continually recommit to serving God. It can't be a one-time thing. Every time you encounter a command or principle in Scripture, trust that God knows best and is worthy of your worship.

Prayer Prompt
"Lord, please convict me when I don't trust Your Word. Show me from the Scriptures how You want me to change."

LifeWork for Your Family

Your strife Creators aren't trusting God. They believe their way is best. Unfortunately, you can't change their beliefs, so you must instead commit to consistently and regularly drawing them back to the trustworthiness of God and His expectations for their lives. Allow the Holy Spirit to do the convicting work you can't do, but don't neglect to play your part. As the apostle Paul sagely explains, "I planted, Apollos watered, but God gave the growth" (I Corinthians 3:6).

There's a dangerous misconception that views faith as a mental (spiritual) exercise that has no direct impact on our decisions—but trust, in fact, *determines* our trajectory. Faith is what makes us function. Belief affects our behavior. I say this because I don't want anyone to be confused into thinking that *trusting* God is a step that can be taken all by itself (without taking the next two steps). Choosing to trust God will necessitate *all* the steps that follow. This reality reveals that if you or anyone in your family is struggling with the following steps, the real issue is that you're not trusting God as you should.

Once we learn to trust that God's will is perfect and must be followed, this revelation will lead us to submit to the Spirit.

2. Submit to the Spirit
If I had all the information necessary to put a man on the moon, I guarantee it would never happen! It can't happen. It doesn't matter what I know about physics, engineering, telemetry, radiation shielding, trigonometry,

gravitational pull, thrust, propulsion, and the many other disciplines necessary to propel someone there and bring them back again safely. In fact, it doesn't matter if I were a genius capable of replacing everyone who works at NASA or SpaceX—it would still not be possible for me to put a man on the moon.

It would be impossible for one important reason: *I don't have the resources*. I don't have the financial buying power. The Planetary Society says that between 1960 and 1973, Project Apollo cost the United States $25.8 billion. They estimate that with inflation, that cost would increase to about $257 billion today. I simply don't have those resources, and I never will in my own power. That's why nations were the first people to send humans into space, and multi-billion dollar companies are the ones sending people to space now. Aaron M. Brewster—regardless of how much he knows and how much faith he has in the science—will never put someone on the moon because he doesn't have the power to do so. This same concept is true concerning our ability to obey God.

To take the first step toward obedience, we need to know, understand, and trust the truth of God—we need to truly *believe* God. Yet knowing and understanding something is pointless if we don't put that information into action. This poses a problem because we don't receive the strength we need to accomplish the things of God from our breakfast cereal. Let's consider what we're able to achieve in our own power. The words of Galatians 5:20 should be familiar to most of us: "[The fruit of the flesh is] idolatry, sorcery, enmity, strife, jealousy, fits of anger, rivalries, dissensions, divisions." These wicked works are all we can accomplish in our own strength, and Romans 8:8 underscores this truth: "Those who are in the flesh cannot please God." It's impossible for a human being to glorify God without the supernatural empowering of the Holy Spirit.

In contrast, Galatians 5:22-23 reveals how the Holy Spirit empowers a believer: "The fruit of the Spirit is love, joy, peace, patience, kindness, goodness, faithfulness, gentleness, self-control; against such things there is no law." But the question then is, Who is the Holy Spirit, and what part does He play in our lives?

Pneumatology, the study of the Holy Spirit, is a wide-ranging field. We don't have the time to go into great detail about the Spirit's role in our lives, and yet it's absolutely vital for us to understand Who He is and what He does, especially if we are to submit to Him. My brief introduction below puts the work of the Spirit into context.

Who Is the Holy Spirit?

The Holy Spirit is just as much God as the Father and the Son. He is spoken of as God and is identified with the title of Yahweh (or Jehovah) (Acts 5:1–4; Isaiah 6:8–9 with Acts 28:25-26; Jeremiah 31:31–34; with Hebrews 10:15-17). We're told that the Christian the Spirit indwells is indwelt by God (I Corinthians 3:16; 6:19; Ephesians 2:22). The Holy Spirit possesses the attributes of deity, such as omniscience, omnipresence, omnipotence, and eternality (I Corinthians 2:10–11; Psalm 139:7; Zechariah 4:6; Hebrews 9:14). He does works only God can do, like creating, regenerating, and sanctifying (Genesis 1:2; John 3:6; II Thessalonians 2:13).

The Holy Spirit is God eternal. He owns the cattle on a thousand hills (Psalm 50:10). He is all-powerful, all-knowing, all-wise, and all-sovereign. This truth should produce infinite confidence the Holy Spirit is abundantly capable of doing everything I can't. Only He can provide the strength to accomplish His will in my life. Knowing this, I can have confidence that He is strong enough to help me navigate the Mushroom Incident to His honor and glory. Knowing how powerful He is, I can have hope when I have an unruly teenager in my life.

But how exactly does His power work in my life?

What Does the Holy Spirit Do?

Going back to the beginning of time, right at the start of the Bible in the second verse of Genesis, we find the Holy Spirit participated in the creation of the world (Genesis 1:2), and He has been active on Earth ever since (Genesis 6:3; Isaiah 40:12-13). This is an important fact to recognize because it gives us hope that new life and maturity are not beyond His scope. The Holy Spirit's role at the beginning of this new life is to convict the world concerning sin, righteousness, and judgment (John 16:7-11). We and our family members require our eyes to be opened to our needs, and we need the Holy Spirit in order to recognize the depth of our spiritual destitution.

Then, when we believe the truth concerning our sin and His holiness, He does something else for us. The Spirit is intimately involved in our salvation (John 3:3-7; Titus 3:5; I Corinthians 12:13; Romans 6:1–10; II Corinthians 1:22; Ephesians 1:13; 4:30). The Father ordained it, the Son gave Himself for it, and the Holy Spirit is the agent Who applies Christ's sacrifice and blessings. This is why it's crucial to recognize that true victory over strife is only accessible to followers of God.

Several Scriptures confirm that once a person submits to follow Christ, the Holy Spirit resides in him (Romans 8:9; I Corinthians 6:19-20, 12:13; Ephesians 4:30; Romans 8:9; Jude 1:19). This indwelling of the Spirit is the very presence of God permanently in and available to us. We don't have to wait in line, and we don't have to fear losing Him. We know that any time we want to rely entirely on God and access His strength to accomplish His will, He is willing and able to meet any requirement we have. Through this indwelling of the Holy Spirit, we receive so many blessings. Jesus Himself referred to the Holy Spirit as the Helper (John 14:16), and Romans 8:26-27 tells us the Holy Spirit helps us in our weakness and explains how He even helps us pray in ways we could never pray on our own.

Of vital importance is knowing that it is the Spirit Who enlightens us to spiritual truth (John 15:26; John 16:13-14; I Corinthians 12:3). This takes us back to the first point: our ability to accurately know and understand the truth of Scripture comes directly from the Holy Spirit. In addition to giving us life and the capacity to understand God's will, the Holy Spirit equips us to serve God and live according to His will (I Corinthians 12; Luke 12:12; I Peter 4:10-11; Ephesians 2:10; Romans 12; Ephesians 4). The fruit of the Spirit is essential for imitating God and thereby replacing the acidic sin in our dams with refreshing righteousness.

The Holy Spirit, however, doesn't just give us gifts and leave us—He empowers us to *use* the gifts to live righteously (Galatians 5:16, 22-23; Romans 12:1-2; Ephesians 5:18; Colossians 3:16). When we are filled with the Spirit we are able to communicate in ways that produce peace. We're able to deny the flesh and accomplish the nine strife-killing character qualities of believing in and loving God, being selfless and loving others, as well as being honest, merciful, humble, wise, and holy.

It's critically important, however, for your family members to recognize that the indwelling of the Holy Spirit is not the same as possession by an evil spirit. People seldom choose to be possessed by a demon, but if they do become possessed, they tend to perform involuntarily wicked acts through that spirit's prompting. Believers are not puppets who involuntarily do everything perfectly all the time. We must choose to be filled with—and therefore controlled by—the Holy Spirit. In Ephesians 5:18, we are commanded to be filled with the Spirit so that He influences everything we do. This is not some mystical act, nor does it require any ritual or rite. It's as easy as recognizing God's expectations for us and then doing them, putting one foot in front of the other and trusting the Spirit to do the rest.

Our choice to submit to the Spirit is clearly illustrated in the Book of Acts. In Acts 4:8, we read, "Then Peter, filled with the Holy Spirit, said to them, ..." What came next was biblical truth spoken for the glory of God, the conviction of sinners, and the edification of God's people. Then, in Acts 5:3, we read, "But Peter said, 'Ananias, why has Satan filled your heart to lie to the Holy Spirit and to keep back for yourself part of the proceeds of the land?'" In Acts 4, Peter submitted to the Spirit, saying and doing that which would please Him, but in Acts 5, Ananias acted in a manner contrary to the will of God and fought the Holy Spirit's work in Him.

Our part is choosing to submit to the work God wants to do in us. We choose to please the Lord and trust the Holy Spirit to empower us to make the necessary changes. Deciding to submit and rely on God's authority can be likened to the engineers and scientists who put the first men on the moon. They trusted that the United States government would pay the bills, so they ordered the materials and built the rocket. The vast majority of them didn't give a second thought to whether or not the government could afford it. They did their job and let the accountants do the rest. In the same way, to end the strife in your family, each of you will have to voluntarily put yourself under the authority and power of God and then trust Him to equip you to do it.

LifeWork for You

Every time you encounter a command or principle in Scripture, trust that God knows best and submit to the Spirit by consciously choosing to obey the command and live the principle: "Submit yourselves therefore to God. Resist the devil, and he will flee from you. 8 Draw near to God, and he will draw near to you. Cleanse your hands, you sinners, and purify your hearts, you double-minded" (James 4:7-8).

Prayer Prompt

"Father, I want to obey You, but I know I can't do it in my own power. As I take this step to submit to You, I thank You for enabling me to do it."

LifeWork for Your Family

Those who create strife in your family aren't presenting themselves as living, holy sacrifices to God (Romans 12:1). You need to help them understand what it means to trust Him so implicitly that they would undertake the most seemingly impossible tasks simply because God commanded it. Such trust and submission can be learned as the Holy Spirit empowers them, but they will still benefit from you teaching them to surrender their will and demonstrating it for them in daily life.

In chapter three, we discussed the Consequences of strife, but there are also consequences of submission. Just as strife creates personal hurt, interpersonal hurt, and divine hurt, submission to God results in personal growth, interpersonal growth, and divine growth. We must remember, though, that spiritual growth is not something that just happens to us. Spiritual growth is the incremental process that results from trusting God and submitting to Him multiple times a day, hundreds of times a week, thousands of times a month, and tens of thousands of times a year. Spiritual growth is a process of deciding—of consciously choosing—to trust God and submit to His Word in every moment.

Trust the Truth and Submit to the Spirit. You cannot submit to the Spirit if you don't trust God's truth, and your family will never accomplish the third and final step in God's Cure for family strife if they aren't pursuing the first two.

We're going to dedicate the whole of the next chapter to the third requirement in God's Cure for strife because I don't want to present what may seem merely like pie-in-the-sky-in-the-great-by-and-by. I want to step through each of the ingredients so we can all appreciate that God intends for us to eat of this "pie" here and now. He created us to live this way, He commands us to live this way, and He capacitates us (through the Spirit) to live this way.

7
Grow in God

In the last chapter we laid out God's first two steps for strifelessness. First, we need to Trust the Truth. Second, we must Submit to the Spirit. Only then will we (and our families) be able to Grow in God. Spiritual growth is absolutely crucial to remove strife from your family circle. However, despite being desperately vital to a family's long-term freedom from strife, spiritual growth follows a simple formula, as described in Ephesians 4:22-24.

1. Put off sin.
2. Renew your mind.
3. Put on righteousness.

Spiritual maturity is the process of working from the general to the specific. As one becomes more specific in any discipline, a greater depth of detail becomes discernible to practitioners within that discipline. That's why we're dedicating a whole chapter to this one step. We need to understand the specific trajectory God has planned for our spiritual maturity before we'll be able to participate in it as we should.

As a biblical counselor, I often find myself turning to II Peter 1:2-10 to explain the process of spiritual growth. While there are any number of passages dealing with this topic, Peter lays out a clear, manageable roadmap that appeals to my sensibilities. Let's start by analyzing the first four verses of the passage:

> Simon Peter, a bond-servant and apostle of Jesus Christ,
> To those who have received a faith of the same kind as ours, by the righteousness of our God and Savior, Jesus Christ: ² Grace and peace be multiplied to you in the knowledge of God and of Jesus our Lord;
> ³ seeing that His divine power has granted to us everything pertaining to life and godliness, through the true knowledge of Him who called us by His own glory and excellence. ⁴ For by these He has granted to us His precious and magnificent promises, so that by them you may become partakers of *the* divine nature, having escaped the corruption that is in the world by lust (II Peter 1:1-4 [NASB 1995]).

The Calling and the Conditions

Peter begins this letter by unveiling the marvelous, hope-giving truth that those who have obtained faith through Christ are now in a position to have God multiply His grace and peace to them. Coupled with this joyous reality, Peter includes a caveat: God's grace and peace are only multiplied in our lives through *the knowledge of God*. He then explains that the knowledge of God contains *everything* we need for life and godliness, enabling us to become partakers of the divine nature so we can accomplish the work to which God has called us.

The tension between divine empowerment and personal responsibility is significant. Leaning too far in either direction creates dangerous results. On one side, it's tempting to "let go and let God," basically living our lives however we want because we have our "fire insurance" against going to hell. If, however, we lean too far into personal responsibility, we run the risk of becoming pharisaical legalists working in our own power for our eternal life. True spiritual maturity is, therefore, the result of us doing our part and trusting God to do His.

The question then becomes, "To what is God calling us?" Verse 4 describes it as becoming partakers of the divine nature and escaping from the world's corruption by lust. Those are the beginning and endpoints of our spiritual maturity. We all start life in this world corrupted by lust, but when we are born again, we are to grow into the divine nature by enjoying God's precious and magnificent promises.

The Path of Growth

Now, let's read verses 5 through 10 and then analyze the beauty of this comprehensive list:

> Now for this very reason also, applying all diligence, in your faith supply moral excellence, and in your moral excellence, knowledge, 6 and in your knowledge, self-control, and in your self-control, perseverance, and in your perseverance, godliness, 7 and in your godliness, brotherly kindness, and in your brotherly kindness, love. 8 For if these qualities are yours and are increasing, they render you neither useless nor unfruitful in the true knowledge of our Lord Jesus Christ. 9 For he who lacks these qualities is blind or short-sighted, having forgotten his purification from his former sins. 10 Therefore, brethren, be all the more diligent to make certain about His calling and choosing you; for as long as you practice these things, you will never stumble (II Peter 1:5-10 [NASB 1995]).

Having established *how* to grow in Christ, Peter reemphasizes in verse 5 the tension between divine enablement and personal responsibility when he commands us to apply "all diligence." The idea of diligence comes up again in verse 10 when he tells us to "be all the more diligent to make certain about His calling and choosing you." Essentially, God wants us to move from strife-creating sinfulness to peace-creating godliness by diligent effort in conjunction with Holy Spirit empowerment. While this big-picture view sounds great, we must understand the *practical* nature of our intended growth. Knowing this, in verses 5 through 7, Peter provides a super-relevant roadmap outlining the attainment of our spiritual growth.

Remember that the information in this chapter—Grow in God—rests on the last two points dealt with in the previous chapter—Trust the Truth, and Submit to the Spirit. As we build on prior knowledge, you will recognize how crucial these building blocks are when applying them to your comprehension of the final chapter (Quit the Strife).

Faith

Spiritual life starts with faith. As we learned in the last chapter, if we want to stem the flow of strife-causing sin in our lives, we must deny deliberate unbelief—the flip side of which is trusting truth. Real growth starts when we choose to believe family strife is entirely unacceptable because it is the result of our sinful choices and that we must do something about it. Recognizing that God is worthy of our worship and capable of helping us quit the strife is our only option for success. Your family will not be able to quit bringing strife into your home if they have not put their trust in Jesus Christ.

Moral Excellence

Why is moral excellence (or virtue) the second item on the list? Wouldn't it make more sense for this subject to be a step further down the line? Isn't moral excellence something into which we have to grow over time? While we don't have time to discuss virtue more extensively, I encourage you to listen to a series I did for *The Celebration of God*. It's called *The Evidence of Spiritual Life*, and it works through each of these maturity milestones in more detail.

For now, though, it's important to note three divine realities concerning moral excellence:

Evidence of Spiritual Life

1. The moment we are born again, we are placed *positionally* into the righteousness of Christ—but there's more.
2. The moment we are born again is the very first moment we are capable of *practically* being morally excellent—but again, there's more.
3. When we are born again, God *expects* us to start living a morally excellent life *immediately*.

Born-again believers don't get to say, "Well, I'm still a baby in Christ, so I don't have to be that good," or "Yes, he says he's a Christian, but he's a teenager, so . . . ."

Nope. All Christians are capable of genuine moral excellence by sheer virtue of the fact that they are Christians. Of course, the maturity process will result in us becoming *more* excellent as we mature, but the expectation is there from the moment we are reborn. This realization is why we must deny immaturity and submit to the Holy Spirit. Your family will not be able to quit strife *if they are not pursuing the moral excellence of God.*

Knowledge

As previously noted, maturity equals specificity. Whether the individual is a professional athlete, astronaut, actor, or accountant, the professional's knowledge base is much broader and deeper than those who are just starting in those same fields. Children come into this world with no concrete information. As they grow, they learn new things and how those truths affect each other. Through that process, they learn to make informed decisions that seek beneficial outcomes instead of harmful consequences. I tell my family all the time, "The more information we have, the better the choices we can make."

The same is true of spiritual growth. Consider Peter's words at the beginning of the passage that opens his second epistle. Grace, peace, and everything we need for life and godliness are only to be found in the *knowledge* of God. The more godly knowledge you possess, the more you seek it out. This fact is why Proverbs 18:15 says, "An intelligent heart acquires knowledge, and the ear of the wise seeks knowledge." We will only grow in Christ if we learn more about Him from His Word, and your family will only be able to quit strife if they are in the habit of reading, studying, and meditating on Scripture.

Self-Control

As we exercise our faith by living the morally right life we know to live and consistently seeking out the knowledge of God so we can grow in our moral excellence, we will have to exercise plenty of self-control. Remember, we were born into the lusts of the flesh in the sin of this world. We're selfish self-worshippers addicted to our own will. Spiritual growth requires learning to deny our flesh, take up our crosses, and follow Jesus (Matthew 16:24; Mark 8:34; Luke 9:23).

Of course, we can't achieve this in our own power, so self-control means submission of self to the Spirit's control. Your family cannot quit strife if they try to do it in their own power and for their own satisfaction. They must submit to the Holy Spirit and choose to cooperate with Him as they say "No" to self and "Yes" to God.

Perseverance

As we take these tiny steps toward spiritual maturity, learning to reject our sinful impulses and put on the righteousness of God, these momentary events will compile until they result in a life well-lived to the glory of God.

This incremental accrual of faith, moral excellence, knowledge, and self-control is why perseverance is desperately necessary for our spiritual growth. We can't stop growing if we're alive. Living things grow, and if we're not growing, it reveals evidence we were never truly alive. We must persevere in our sanctification and conformity to the image of Jesus Christ because we have eternal spiritual life that will continue through the ages. Your family will not be able to quit strife if they are not steadfastly and consistently pursuing spiritual maturity.

Godliness

What is the result of our spiritual growth? II Peter 1:4 describes the benefit of our spiritual maturity as partaking in the divine nature. Hebrews 12:10b explains it this way, "That we may share his holiness." Ephesians 4:13 couches it in these words: "Until we all attain to the unity of the faith and of the knowledge of the Son of God, to mature manhood, to the measure of the stature of the fullness of Christ." In II Peter 1:7, the author describes it simply as "godliness."

Godliness refers to a Godward inclination that results in a godlike life. This process doesn't mean we become gods, but it does mean we grow into that godlike image God originally instilled within mankind. It means that these steps of faith, moral excellence, knowledge, self-control, and perseverance aren't defined by what *we* want but conform to *His* will. It's what Paul is talking about in Romans 8:29a when he wrote, "For those whom he foreknew he also predestined to become conformed to the image of his Son."

Becoming more Christ-like is the goal toward which all Christians are growing, and it's the purpose for the power God so graciously offers us. Our constant striving to imitate Jesus is the reason Peter included godliness as something to attain on our journey of spiritual growth: "His divine power has granted to us all things that pertain to life and **godliness**, through the knowledge of him who called us to his own glory and excellence" (II Peter 1:3 —my emphasis). Godliness is the goal, and *godliness is a strife-killer*. It's the only strife-killer. Your family will not be able to quit strife if they aren't following the pattern of spiritual growth laid out in Romans 12:1-2:

> I appeal to you therefore, brothers, by the mercies of God, to present your bodies as a living sacrifice, holy and acceptable to God, which is your spiritual worship. 2 Do not be conformed to this world, but be **transformed** by the renewal of your mind, that by testing you may discern what is the will of God, what is good and acceptable and perfect (Romans 12:1-2—my emphasis).

Brotherly Kindness

The final two line items on Peter's pathway to spiritual maturity, brotherly kindness and love, are slightly different from the rest of the list.

Faith leads to excellence, which leads to a desire to know more about God. This desire leads to exercising self-control to submit to God's expectations, leading (over time) to perseverance, resulting in godliness. At this point, Peter zooms in—he gets more *specific*—about what godliness actually looks like in daily life. These final two practical, outward expressions of godliness create an atmosphere where strife disintegrates and melts away.

Brotherly kindness is a facet of divine love that emphasizes the relational necessity of spiritual growth. The New Testament has over thirty unique commands, often called the one-anothers. These commands are "the work of ministry" our pastors should be equipping us to perform so we can build the body of Christ (Ephesians 4:11-12). They involve us interacting with each other in intentional, conscious, life-on-life ways designed to result in all believers attaining "to the unity of the faith and of the knowledge of the Son of God, to mature manhood, to the measure of the stature of the fullness of Christ" (Ephesians 4:13). They're all necessary outward expressions of brotherly kindness.

God created us to thrive in community. What better nuclear example of this truth is there than the family? It starts with a husband and wife living in community as ambassadors of God's gospel-rooted relationship with His people. A married couple's community multiplies as they have children, who they raise in a godly manner, constantly working to introduce their kids to God and further disciple them in His ways. This family nucleus is the perfect environment for peace, love, joy, encouragement, and friendship to flourish. It is the very antithesis of strife. Without this godly environment, your family will not be able to quit strife because they haven't received the tools to know, understand, and exercise brotherly love.

Love

Whereas brotherly kindness focuses on the relational aspect of biblical love, the Greek word translated as "love" in II Peter 1:7 focuses on the personal responsibility we have to love others *even when those around us aren't participating*.

Strife is possible when only one person is thundering their acidic sinfulness onto the people around them. This person can—all by themselves—increase their strife by adding more sins and compounding more transgression. However, the moment another person in the family retaliates in sin—creating their own strife in the situation—the strife isn't just added; it's *multiplied*. The more people who participate in the strife, the faster it multiplies. You know this to be true. You've experienced it.

The ultimate strife-*divider* is biblical love because love refuses to sin against another. It refuses to multiply the strife crashing around the room, and it can do so by the power of God even when no one else is participating.

I want to encourage you once again to have your family listen to the *Family Love Series,* because it works through the bulk of what the Bible has to say on the subject of love.

One of the most challenging elements within this subject is the idea of loving one's enemy. It comes down to choosing to want God's best interest in your enemy's life and to work toward this end even when they don't deserve it, despite them hating you for it. Your family cannot quit strife if they don't learn to love the other family members, even if that means loving the strife-causers.

Family Love Series

Learning this lesson has come at an all-too-painful price in my own life. I have far too often justified being unloving to friends and family members who I thought "deserved it." But my hatred did nothing more than exacerbate and multiply the problem. It wasn't until God pierced my heart and showed me that I wasn't loving Him because I wasn't loving those "enemies" that I started to understand how unjustifiable it is to treat someone poorly because they treat you poorly. I'm definitely not perfect in this respect, but I praise God for how far I've come learning to love those who don't love me back. And I could never have done it without studying the Scriptures to learn how to love the way God loves us.

Reading this book, listening to sermons, and studying the Bible exposes you to the truth that God expects you to believe, ultimately resulting in you growing in that truth. It's important to remember, though, you'll never grow in that truth if you're not submitting to the power and authority of the Holy Spirit in your life. Yet, as you trust, submit, and grow, you will find it increasingly easier to quit the strife in your home.

LifeWork for You

1. Are you a student of the Word?   Yes   No

2. When you encounter commands and principles, do you actively try to understand those principles or commands so you can put them into practice in your life?   Yes   No

3. When was the last time you changed how you live because of what you encountered in the Bible?

_____

_____

_____

4. When you do change because of the Scriptures, are you doing so to the honor and glory of God through the power of God? Or are you trying to do it in your own strength because you think you'll like the benefit it will provide you? How can you know for sure?

_____

_____

_____

_____

Prayer Prompt

"Dear Lord, I can't mature in Christ without Your truth and empowerment. Please open my eyes so I may behold wondrous things out of Your Law and use those wondrous things to transform me into the image of Your Son. As I obey You, empower my steps so I may persevere in godliness."

LifeWork for Your Family

Your strife Creators need to be spiritually mature. They need the gospel's truth in salvation and sanctification, and they need your brotherly kindness as you help sharpen them in their relationship with God. Don't take spiritual growth for granted because physical development seems to happen without your involvement. Everyone needs to purposefully engage with those who will speak truth into their lives so they can be matured and built up in love (Ephesians 4:15-16; James 5:13-20).

I want to share a secret with you. This book isn't really about how to cure strife. Yes, submitting to the biblical truth we've covered will definitely put an end to the strife in your home. But this book is actually about *family discipleship*. The process of growing away from sin and toward righteousness is the very definition of sanctification, and the process whereby friends and families help each other grow in their sanctification is called discipleship.

It just so happens that strife is one of the most obvious indicators that one or more people in a home are either not born again, or they have a lot of important growing to do in their walk with the Lord. So, this book is actually just an introduction to biblical discipleship with a beautiful revelation of the peace and harmony it brings.

We've been talking about what it is to know and understand God and His will for our lives and then how to put that into practice in our homes . . . yes, so that we will have less strife, but . . . even more so . . . so that God's will for our conformity to Jesus Christ will be achieved and He will be glorified. The more you are conformed to the image of Jesus Christ, the easier it will be to follow our four necessary steps: *Trust, Submit, Grow,* and, having done the work necessary, you and your family will finally be able to *Quit* the strife that plagues you.

But since this is an introduction to the necessary steps for discipleship and—by no means—a silver bullet or magical potion, it's important that we know how God wants us daily teaching and reproving and correcting and training our strife Creators. So, the next chapter is going to discuss how to help our family members mature in Christ so we can all enjoy a home with less strife and more love.

8
Quit the Strife

How can your family put a final end to all the strife within the family circle? Previous chapters have taught us to trust God, submit to Him, and grow in Him—so what's this final step? How does it complement and complete the trifecta of trust, submission, and growth?

Suppose I were sitting across from your entire family, and we had all read and understood the first seven chapters of this book. This is what I would probably say: "The final step to ending strife in your home is simple: if you are all trusting God's plan, submitting to His power, and growing in your maturity, all you have to do is *stop sinning against each other*. When you do that, the strife will vanish. Do right. Quit doing wrong. It is truly that simple."

Just stop sinning?

Quit the strife?

Can it truly be that simple?

Suppose everyone in your family understood God's expectations and submitted to His Spirit as they matured in their faith. In that case, you would all increasingly choose Christ-honoring ways of responding to each other. When Christ is honored, strife becomes non-existent.

Every person in the home is, however, responsible for their own choices. Your kids can't make you change, and you can't force your kids to grow. Thankfully, even if your family members refuse to trust, submit, and mature, *you* can still do something about yourself. God calls everyone in the home to participate in this process, both children and parents. Because this book focuses primarily on spouses and parents, I will explain every step with examples relevant to spouses and parents, but all of these truths apply just as much if you happen to be one of the children or if you're experiencing strife with a friend.

We know God expects adults in a family to shine the light of the gospel, which includes both evangelism and discipleship. God commands His people to "Go therefore and make disciples of all nations" (Matthew 28:19a). Jesus later clarified this directive shortly before His ascension, saying, "You will be my witnesses in Jerusalem and in all Judea and Samaria, and to the end of the earth" (Acts 1:8). Jerusalem was considered the hub of the nation, while Judea encompassed the surrounding areas. Although Samaria was technically part of Israel, the Jews viewed it as a stain on their nation. It was geographically included but culturally excluded because of their heritage and worship choices. And the "end of the earth" was a term used for everywhere else.

Notice how the Great Commission begins at home and then extends outward. Consider that the first created institution of man was the home. It came before organized religion and way before government. God's first expectation for pastors is that they have everything in order at home. God's expectation for the family includes all the direct scriptural commands for how we live and interact within our family group. I highlight this to emphasize *our divine calling from God* to actively be salt and light in our homes. We have no excuse to abdicate that calling. Once we trust the truth and submit to it, we must grow in our ability to fulfill our divine calling—but how do we activate this spiritual influence in our home?

This final section focuses on the biblical means of influencing your children and spouse to better know, understand, and serve God—thus decreasing the strife in your home. This book's length, designed to be short and easily consumable, leaves much more to say on the subject of discipleship, so I encourage you to check out our *Biblical Parenting Essentials Conference* in the Evermind App. By scanning the QR code you can access the conference *free of charge!*

This six-part parenting conference explores in more detail each of the steps outlined below. You'll also receive access to many more resources to help you expand your knowledge of the elements presented. Follow these steps to register and download the app.
1. Scan the code.
2. Create your free account login and password.
3. Update your name and picture in the community tab.
4. Enjoy the conference!

The Necessary Foundation

To parent your children in eternally beneficial ways, you must believe you're an ambassador for God, called by Him to represent Him in your home, as detailed in scripture:

> Therefore, if anyone is in Christ, he is a new creation. The old has passed away; behold, the new has come. [18] All this is from God, who through Christ reconciled us to himself and gave us the ministry of reconciliation; [19] that is, in Christ God was reconciling the world to himself, not counting their trespasses against them, and entrusting to us the message of reconciliation.

[20] Therefore, we are ambassadors for Christ, God making his appeal through us. We implore you on behalf of Christ, be reconciled to God.
II Corinthians 5:17-20

This reconciliation process is why Christian parents must bring their children up "in the discipline and instruction of the Lord" (Ephesians 6:4). It's aimed at helping to reconcile them with God. If your kids are not born again, this reconciliation takes the form of Evangelism Parenting because you realize that without Christ, your children have no hope in this life or the one to come. When your children put their faith in God to save them from their sins and enter into an eternal relationship with Him, you can start implementing Discipleship Parenting.

Both parenting styles require us to root all our parenting actions in the Bible because God has chosen to reveal Himself to us through Scripture. He's specifically crafted His holy Word to teach us about His nature, call us to Him, help us turn from ourselves, and continue growing in Him. It is, therefore, our responsibility as His ambassadors to speak His Word into every facet of our parenting. This responsibility includes weaving God's Word into life's "mundane" things like vegetables, chores, homework, TV, and sports. All aspects of life must be founded on Scripture, but how do we use the Bible to bring our kids up in the nurture and admonition of the Lord?

II Timothy 3:16-17 has the answer: "All Scripture is breathed out by God and profitable for teaching, for reproof, for correction, and for training in righteousness, [17] that the man of God may be complete, equipped for every good work."

Evangelism Parenting

Discipleship Parenting

The Point of Nearly Every Conversation

Teaching

Biblical teaching uses God's Word to help our children know, understand, and believe what God says concerning right and wrong. *The Point of Nearly Every Conversation* in our homes should be to draw the minds of our children back to the truth about God, His Word, and ourselves, prompting them to decide whether or not they choose to believe what God has said. Do you see how the first step in curing strife—trust—is intrinsically tied to the first step of parenting? We must teach our children to trust everything God says in His Word, but when do we start this process?

People have a strange habit of reacting poorly to a crisis rather than preparing a reasonable response to a potential problem . . . in advance. Most people will only work on their cars once there's a problem. According to the Census Bureau, in 2021, thirty million Americans didn't have medical insurance, and this is how we often handle our parenting choices. If there isn't an identifiable problem, we assume everything is working as it should—but this assumption couldn't be further from the truth.

We're all sinners! In one way or another, we're all under perpetual temptation from Satan, the World, and our Flesh. To better equip you to combat the enemy, check out *The Spiritual Warfare in Your Home Series.*

The Spiritual Warfare in Your Home

Once an issue is outwardly manifested, you've already waited too long. You must teach your kids about God, His Word, and themselves long before they're experiencing a meltdown in the grocery store. You must teach your kids about sin, righteousness, temptation, and obedience *before* they hit each other, steal, lie, or swear. Just because they're not acting this way now doesn't mean they won't suffer temptation in the future. Christ-honoring parenting will prepare your kids to be successful when the temptation comes. We must, therefore, teach our children these truths immediately. Most parents will only pick up a book about family strife or look for a biblical counselor once they lose control of an already bad situation. Surely a family would experience a better outcome if the parents had started *preemptively* laying the necessary groundwork for a Christ-honoring, strife-free home years before? So, whether your home is relatively strife-free or plagued by strife, don't wait until the next dam explodes before addressing the issue. Start now. Weave the truths about God, faith, excellence, knowledge, self-control, perseverance, godliness, brotherly kindness, and love into the tapestry of your lives. Hold each other accountable to submit to God's expectations.

Have you memorized our theme verse yet? "The beginning of strife is like letting out water, so quit **before** the quarrel breaks out" (Proverbs 17:14 —my emphasis). Another relevant Scripture to bear in mind is Proverbs 20:3, which says, "It is an honor for a man to keep **aloof** from strife, but every fool will be quarreling" (my emphasis). We, our spouses, and our children must work daily on closing the pipeline releasing sin into our dams. The best way to guarantee our dam walls will never break (resulting in strife) is to make sure there's as little pressure and temptation from our sinful flesh as possible. This protective mechanism requires trusting truth, submitting to the Spirit, and growing in God *before* an issue develops.

Of course, this doesn't mean you stop speaking the truth when your children or spouse are in the midst of sinning. You must continue teaching even if strife is currently pouring, although it tends not to be as valuable as starting sooner. Purposeful, premeditated, preemptive parenting is so much better than finding yourself on your heels, painted into a corner, between a rock and a hard place, or other uncomfortable metaphors.

On the other hand, what if you've done the daily work of teaching your kids truth, but they still don't believe it? What if their actions, words, emotions, and desires reveal they don't trust God's way is best?

Reproving

When your children inevitably reveal they don't trust God's plan for their lives, you must turn to God-given Scripture to reprove them. If teaching is communicating to our kids what is right and wrong, then reproof is convincing our kids what they did, said, felt, wanted, or believed is wrong.

This step can't be about your opinion versus theirs. It must be based on *what God says* is right and wrong. It's our job as Ambassadors for Yahweh to use Scripture to persuasively show our children that they misinterpreted what they should have done in the moment and that God's plan was best all along. Parents must reteach them what they must do (and say, feel, desire, and believe) the next time they encounter a similar situation. Too often, parents don't preemptively teach their children, so the only parenting tool they have is to reprove them after the fact. Reproof is essential, but it's far more powerful when we've laid a solid foundation by teaching them God's way beforehand.

When you explain to your children what they did was wrong, you can mention previous truths you've taught your family:

> "Do you remember discussing how God wants you to do your best in everything? Do you remember what we've learned about true

Consequences

obedience? Your choice to cut corners on your chore and disregard how your parents told you to do it has resulted in exactly what God promised—consequences. You've hurt yourself by building destructive habits, damaged your fellowship with us by sinning against us, and hurt your fellowship with God by sinning against Him. You would have avoided all these negative consequences had you trusted and submitted to God's plan."

At this point, real-time consequences come into effect. Remember, reproof is about persuasively helping your children recognize God is right and they were wrong. You might remember that consequences are the unavoidable reality of the universe God created. But be aware that it is possible to apply inappropriate or incorrect repercussions, so make sure the consequences you choose conform to God's Word on every point. The Bible has everything we need for life and godliness, so draw from Scripture in your application.

It's wonderful when our kids respond to biblical parenting in humble contrition, but let's consider what we should do if they *don't* recognize their sin and respond accordingly. What does ambassadorial parenting look like when our kids reject our teaching? Reproof.

What does ambassadorial parenting look like when our kids reject our reproof? More teaching and reproof. It's impossible to move into the third and fourth phases of biblical parenting if our kids don't believe the truth, submit to it, and grow in it. This fact is an unfortunate reality, but if our kids continue to be addicted to their own desires, they will hate God and others. This addiction will cause them to greedily use everything in their arsenal (including dishonesty and anger) to pridefully and foolishly pursue their sin. The pursuit of sin will always result in strife.

So, what's a Christ-honoring parent to do? Be faithful. Be steadfast. Persevere. As you grow in Christ by trusting His truth and submitting to the Holy Spirit, you must be faithful, continuing to parent your children in godly ways. Too many parents eventually give up and retreat from the strife, but this failure does not promote brotherly kindness and love. It doesn't encourage godliness. It reveals selfishness and self-preservation. This failure will cause as much strife as the inconsolable elementary student who wants the new download or the rebellious teenager who hates your rules. We must faithfully teach and reprove, teach and reprove, teach and reprove, and trust God to do what we cannot.

If you're in this situation with your kids—the maelstrom of never-ending teaching and reproof—please involve other believers. Find mature Christians to speak truth into your life, help lift up your arms, and counsel you. At the same time, continue to surround your children with mature believers who will speak truth to them in love. Too often embarrassed parents don't just run from their kids; they run from their church family. Too often, discouraged parents give in to their children, allowing them to listen to ungodly music or attend a school that doesn't align with Christian values. Another problem discouraged parents face is allowing their children to hang out with ungodly "friends." Those of who have listened to TLP's *Friend Series* understand the importance of a biblical understanding of true friendship.

Friends

These parental failures (and more) remove God's salt and light from the family home, ultimately multiplying strife. If you fall into this category, please seek help from a pastor, biblical counselor, and godly friend.

If, however, by the grace of God, your child heeds your reproof, is convinced they have done wrong, and accepts God's will is best, they're ready to cross the bridge to the third stage of ambassadorial parenting influence. Only when the individual chooses to believe the truth, acknowledge his sin, plead forgiveness, and commit to repentance, can you move into the next phase. The Biblical Parenting Essentials Conference goes into more detail about crossing this bridge. For example, you will learn that saying, "I'm sorry," is not an apology. Sorrow alone isn't guaranteed to lead to repentance. Only once the child confesses, apologizes, and begins forsaking their sin are they ready for the correction phase.

Correcting

Correction is the process of returning to the place you should never have left. This concept most closely aligns with the biblical picture of repentance. If I should be walking south, but I'm walking north instead, I need to stop moving north, turn around 180 degrees, and head south. The only way to correct my wrong trajectory is to repent—to turn around.

Repentance, though, is seldom as cut and dried as the process described above. How do you turn south if you don't have a compass? What if it's too hot down south, or there's a giant ravine blocking your way? What if someone promised to give you a million dollars if you keep walking a few

Correct My Child?

more miles north? What if they threaten to kill you if you turn around? These examples more accurately illustrate the difficulty of your children's struggles as they engage with correction.

In a parenting podcast entitled *How Does God Want Me to Correct My Child?* I explain the biblical path to repentance. The section below is adapted from the podcast:

The Bible frequently distinguishes between right and wrong. It becomes relatively easy to reprove using biblical information when we see someone engaging in something the Bible calls sin. Using the Bible to help people correct their trajectory, however, is more complex.

Consider this extreme example. Let's say—God forbid—one of your children engages in homosexual behavior. Most Christians who know their Bible can teach their child that homosexuality is a sin and reprove them if they engage in it. The Bible is clear about sinful actions and motivations and explains what our efforts and incentives should be.

Yet, what are we to do when, after confessing their sin, the child asks how they're supposed to change? We can say, "Well, don't engage in homosexuality," but how do we help the child concerning the practical steps they must take when tempted? What are they to do when they feel an attraction to someone of the same sex? What are the implications for their friend group and entertainment choices?

The Bible does give guidance regarding these questions because God's Word is sufficient for our life and godliness, but it takes someone mature in the Word who can help in applying this guidance.

It's easy to read Ephesians 4:28 to our children: "Let the thief no longer steal, but rather let him labor, doing honest work with his own hands, so that he may have something to share with anyone in need." This biblical advice provides the general trajectory for correction, but what do I tell my child about how to respond to the temptation to steal? Searching for the word "steal" in my Bible won't provide that answer. I have to know what the Bible says about temptation in general.

I can start with James 1 to teach them the difference between temptation and sin. I can then move to I Corinthians 10:13 to help them understand God will always provide a way to escape temptation. Then—depending on the individual's unique needs—I may take them to Philippians 4 to help them address their thought life. Or I may take them to Proverbs 1, which details the consequences of sinful companions, and then guide them to Ecclesiastes to learn about the joy of Christ-honoring friends. Maybe I'll take them to I Corinthians 13 because they need to learn how to love their neighbor better—and thereby stop desiring to take from them.

This correction stage—this *counseling* stage—will require something new from us parents. Sometimes correction is easy and straightforward, and the child—by the grace of God—will renew their mind, put off their sin, and put on Christ's righteousness. Often, though, many questions and related topics are involved in correction. We must be able to guide our children to those biblical truths to help them genuinely return to the safety of God's harbor.

Many biblical parents have come to learn that the correction stage is the most challenging parenting stage. It requires deep biblical understanding and a theological view of life to do it well, but our parents and/or churches have *not* adequately equipped most of us to do it well. This lack is why we must pursue spiritual growth to influence our kids in increasingly godly ways. When we fulfill our ambassadorial responsibility to influence our children with the Word of God, we will teach and reprove them. When they participate in the process, we can also correct them. Then, by the grace of God, we can start training them.

Training

The training stage is one of the easiest. Until now, we've been developing good habits within our children, teaching them what the Bible says about trust, submission, and growth. When they've rebelled, we've reproved them using Scripture. By God's grace, when they've rededicated to trusting, submitting, and growing, we've used the Word to help them correct their trajectory. The training stage involves using the Bible (as we have throughout the process) to support our children as they continue to trust God, submit, and grow in Him.

Because we've cycled through these first three steps until our children understood and practiced them, the Training Stage—much like the concept of perseverance—is the consistent teaching that helps our family members continue quitting strife by following after their Creator. Consider James 1:25, "But one who looks intently at the perfect law, the law of liberty, and abides by it, not having become a forgetful hearer but an effectual doer, this man will be blessed in what he does" (NASB 1995). If you want your kids to be blessed in what they do, they must look intently into God's perfect Law. When they encounter commands, principles, and glimpses of God, they must not merely hear the truth; they must take the information and apply it to their lives as an effectual doer. Training requires us to present Scripture to our children so they—of their own accord—learn, understand, and practice what they find in God's Word.

LifeWork for You

Are you trusting truth, submitting to the Spirit, growing in grace, and stopping the strife? If not, work backward through the list to discover the root problem. The main issue will likely be a key command or principle you're not obeying in daily life. Find guidance. Study the Word and be an effectual doer of it.

Prayer Prompt
"Lord, I create strife because I do not depend on the Holy Spirit to deny myself, take up my cross, and follow You. I'm not submitting to You because I don't believe You're serious about me trusting and obeying You. Please forgive me and show me how I must change."

LifeWork for Your Family

Let's say you aren't a source of strife because you're consistently growing. Wonderful! How can you better influence your family members for Christ? Do you preemptively teach them using the Word of God? Are you faithful to reprove your kids using Scripture? What about correction? Are you providing them with detailed counsel and enforcing accountability? In which of these stages do you need the most work?

The Biblical Parenting Essentials Conference will help you to identify and address how you can better influence your children as an Ambassador of God. Also, you can always contact our biblical counselors at Counselor@TruthLoveParent.com for personalized help.

Conclusion

Have you ever reached the closing day of a week-long conference, looked back, and tried to summarize the scope of everything you were taught in just a few sentences? How do you include all the realizations you had and all the things you now perceive differently? It's difficult. In fact, it's impossible to do the week-long experience justice in only a few sentences or even paragraphs.

So, what do we do now at the end of this study? What are our takeaways? What were the ah-ha moments? What needs to be done differently? Please allow me to attempt to summarize my personal journey through this material. I believe it will provide you with a starting place for harnessing the momentum of this study and allowing it to spin out into your family life.

1. The Creators of Strife

It's easy for me to see all the ways *other* people fail. As with the keen eye of Sherlock Holmes, I can painlessly spot all the ways that other people are causing problems. But I needed to be reminded of two important lessons. First, I will never be any help in a strife-ridden situation if I try to get everything to work out the way *I* want it to work out. I will only increase the strife when I try to accomplish my desires for *my* reasons. Instead, I need to see the problem and the solution as God sees it. The issue isn't my discomfort. It's not that my family isn't living the way I want them to live. The real issue is that we all fail God by trying to dethrone Him.

The second lesson I needed to remember is that even though God would use me to help other people learn about Him, understand Him, and submit to Him, the biggest responsibility in my life is that I know, understand, and obey Him *myself*. I need to deal with the forest of logs lodged in my own eyes before God can use me to deal with the splinters in others' eyes.

The Chief of Sinners

Regardless of who we are, we should all be able to say, "I am the chief of strife Creators in my home." That's where I need to start this process, and that's where you need to start this process. If you are having a hard time imagining that you are the chief of sinners in your home, please listen to the Truth.Love.Parent. podcast episode entitled *The Chief of Sinners in Your Home*.

2. The Consequences of Strife

We've all experienced (or are currently experiencing) the consequences of strife. However, the length, breadth, and depth of the strife shouldn't be our focus. Focusing on the problem produces discontentment, complaining, and despair. For me, I needed to stop looking at the consuming wave of acid and put my eyes back on Christ. I needed to see how our family strife affected God and our fellowship with Him. I needed to understand how God wanted to use the strife in my family to draw us closer to Him and to each other. I needed the hope of God's sovereign plan to reenergize me to approach the situation in His ways for His glory alone.

3. The Causes of Strife

Just like I needed to understand the Consequences of strife through God's eyes, I also needed to trust the Bible's diagnosis of the problem. I spent too much time thinking that the problem was everyone else's inability to simply realize I was right. In reality, I needed to recognize that deliberate unbelief, spiritual immaturity, and fleshly living were the root causes of my family's strife. I couldn't fix something in my own life or assist someone in addressing it in his or her life if I didn't first understand what the real problems were. Our flesh wants to trust our own way above God's (deliberate unbelief), and therefore we pursue our own satisfaction (spiritual immaturity) by living however we feel is right (fleshly living). When I recognized what my wife, my kids, and I needed, it was much easier to start addressing the real problem.

4. The Cure for Strife

Once I truly saw the Creators, Consequences, and Causes of our strife through God's eyes, the Cure made all the sense in the world. Once I recognized the divine enablement promised as I pursued God's Cures, I stopped feeling discouraged, afraid, angry, and depressed. I had hope that peace was truly achievable in and through and for God.

If my family's core attack against the Lord is that we deliberately chose to trust ourselves over His perfect way, we needed to learn to trust God. That meant we needed to go back to the drawing board. We needed to study Who He is and grow in our comprehension of the ramifications of Who He is. He truly is the most trustworthy Person in the cosmos, and when we know Him, we can't help but trust Him.

Yet, my family also needed to grow in Christ. It's not enough to simply say it. It's not enough to say, "The Brewster family believes in God." We needed to *act on that belief*. We needed to have faith that produced moral excellence, knowledge, self-control, perseverance, godliness, brotherly kindness, and love. If those attributes aren't present and progressing in our lives, we don't really trust God the way we think we do, and strife will never cease.

And then, I needed to understand how to set my whole family up for success. I needed to biblically approach the sins that were underlying the strife. I needed to teach my family about God and His expectations for us and reprove them by helping them see how they failed God (not me). During those blessed times when they chose to submit to God's truth, I needed to help them take the practical steps necessary to change, and then I needed to continue helping them embrace that change as they grew increasingly mature. My kids needed that process, my wife needed that process, and I needed that process.

5. Conclusion

But the Brewster's didn't only need that process in the past tense. We still need it in the present and will also need it in the future. This is a process. So, allow me to finish with two of the most important truths I learned (and am learning) through this process.

First, it's never good enough to simply learn. I have to actively live what I've learned. Yes, you can learn a lot throughout a week-long conference, but if you don't implement what you learned and continue implementing it, you will soon find yourself right back where you started . . . or worse. Whether participating in the LifeWork from this book or scouring the Scriptures for practical commands you can start implementing, you have to do something today, tomorrow, and every day to follow.

Second, I need help. I need God's help, but I also need His people's help. Pastors, disciplers, and biblical counselors are designed by God to be a vital part of our faith, maturity, and righteous living. We're not trusting God and His plan if we're too proud, ashamed, or afraid to invite God's people into the process. That will only lead to more strife because it's rooted in deliberate unbelief. That will only ever produce spiritual immaturity and fleshly living.

You can always contact us if you believe you have no one else who can help. We would be honored to help your family quit the strife by becoming the people God called and created you to be. He's still doing that in the Brewster's lives, and I know He wants to do it in yours.

Have hope, my friend. There is a Cure for your family's strife.

Please enjoy these other resources from Evermind Ministries.

This course provides you 25 days of devotional readings, prayer prompts, and unique assignments to help you become the premeditated parent God called and created you to be.

This course includes 9 sessions. Each session is similar to the first half of a biblical counseling session where the family will learn desperately important truths from the book of Ephesians concerning true family unity.

This course includes 12 sessions that will equip God's people to practically glorify Him in their loss, pain, and struggle.

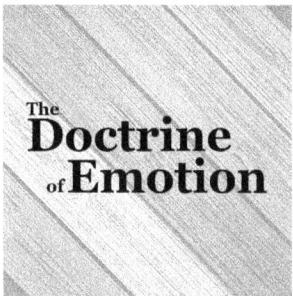 

This course includes 4 units. The first unit deals with what the Bible has to say about emotions in general. The second unit dives into the topics of sorrow, fear, anger, and depression. The third unit includes interviews in which AMBrewster discusses emotions and answers questions. The fourth unit contains workshops Aaron has taught for the Association of Certified Biblical Counselors that deal with the topic of emotions and the Bible.

This course includes sessions on The Purpose of Parenting, The Five Types of Parents, Teaching & Reproof, Correcting & Training, two Practical Q&A sessions, and you will also gain access to an expertly curated set of Biblical Parenting Essential resources to continue your study.

AMBrewster is a follower of Christ, husband to Johanna, father to Micah and Ivy, and eternal delight to the family's Rottweiler, Éowyn.

Aaron is the president of Evermind Ministries, director of Truth.Love.Family., and host of its award-winning parenting podcast, Truth.Love.Parent. He's also an ACBC certified biblical counselor, preacher, speaker, and author. 100% of his time is dedicated to training parents, pastors, counselors, youth workers, and teachers to biblically disciple children and families. His counseling specialities include marriage, at-risk children, families-in-crisis, and Christ-honoring sexuality.

Aaron has created hundreds of hours of free parenting resources including The Celebration of God, a dynamic discipleship experience that equips families to better know, love, and serve the Lord every day of their lives.

The Year Long Celebration of God

www.ingramcontent.com/pod-product-compliance
Lightning Source LLC
Chambersburg PA
CBHW060203050426
42446CB00013B/2972